GOOD HOUSEKEE

PAKISTANI COOKERY

MEERA TANEJA

EBURY PRESS LONDON

Published by Ebury Press
National Magazine House
72 Broadwick Street
London W1V 2BP

First impression 1985
Second impression 1985

ISBN 0 85223 490 2

Designed by Grahame Dudley
Artist Thao Soun
Photography Paul Kemp; stylist Mary Jane Kemp

Illustration on the cover: Chicken Tikka, French beans in Yogurt,
Aromatic Spice Pullao, Chappatis

The Publishers would like to thank
Popatlal Karamshi, 318 Edgeware Road, London W2
for their help in providing props for photography.

Phototypeset by MS Filmsetting Limited, Frome, Somerset
Printed in Great Britain at the University Press, Cambridge

Contents

Introduction

The cooking traditions of the Indian sub-continent, which until 1947 was one country, go back a few thousand years and it would indeed be very difficult to split the culture into Indian or Pakistani as the people are so intermingled. Partition divided not only the land into three divisions, but also split the people. Now half a family may live in Pakistan, the other half in India and a few in Bangladesh.

The cuisine of Pakistan is, of course, as diverse as that of India. Muslim families from all over India travelled to the New Country to set up homes and start a new life, just like the Hindu families left Pakistan to start a new life in India. My own father's family left Lahore to settle in Delhi, but with them they took their traditions, culture and, of course, food. Now there are families all over Pakistan who have origins in South India, Hyderabad, Central India, Bengal, Punjab and the West Coast. Living as they do amongst people of different backgrounds, religions and food habits, these people have invariably learned and adapted them to suit their own life style.

That's how it is with food in Pakistan. Although Muslims are non-vegetarian, it is contrary to popular belief that they do not eat vegetables or pulses and beans. The repertoire of Pakistani food is very similar to that of India; the one difference that springs to mind is that in Pakistani cuisine a lot more cooking fat is used and a fair amount of chilli powder and it is this that gives the food an extremely rich colour. In this book I have reduced the quantities of chilli powder to suit all tastes. After all, it is easier to add more if required than to remove an excess.

Pakistan, although not as large as India, can still be divided into various regions. The extreme north borders on Afghanistan and this country has had a considerable influence on its style of cooking. The people of Peshawar, known as Pathans, are a sturdy breed and are extremely handsome with pale skins, light hair and blue eyes. It would be advisable not to cross a rugged Pathan in an argument! They are an intensely loyal people who take a pride in their culture. The food of this region is mainly non-vegetarian as the climate is extreme and in winter is particularly cold. Murree, with its simply breathtaking scenic beauty, can only be compared with Switzerland, and it was there and in Rawalpindi that I tasted some of the most delicious Kashmiri food.

As I mentioned earlier, my parents came from Lahore and, indeed, it was lucky that my father was transferred back to Karachi to work at the Indian High Commission. For my parents this was just like returning home as happy memories and old friends came flooding back. For me it was an experience in a different way; as a teenager I was the only Hindu girl studying in a convent school and my education came from different directions. Karachi for me was a great place to be in as friends would invite me to their homes only to find me talking to their mothers, grandmothers and, indeed, to their cooks about the art of cooking Muslim food. Karachi, like Delhi, boasted of super little roadside vendors selling all sorts of mouth-watering foods, which of course we used to sneak out of school to eat. It was here that my awareness and interest in different foods developed.

In Lahore I found some of the most delicious tandoori cooking and some Sindhi food, which is not unlike that of India. Some of my own relatives, who are from Sindh, cook exactly the same type of food. As there is a substantial Parsee community in Karachi, it was there that I tasted my first Dhan Sakh.

One particular incident that stands out in my mind was attending the wedding of an extremely rich family. The feasting simply went on for days on end, and nothing amazed me more than the lavish scale of the endless amount of meals that were served, where each dish was even better than the one that went before.

Cooking Equipment

Very few special utensils are needed for cooking Pakistani food. Pots and pans found in most western homes are quite adequate. Even so, it is always exciting to know about and, if you wish, to cook with specialised Pakistani equipment.

Tava: Breads such as chappatis, rotis and parathas are all made on this heavy cast-iron sheet which looks similar to the griddle used for making scones. Any ordinary heavy frying pan makes a good alternative.

Karhai: This is used mainly for deep frying. It looks like a Chinese wok but is heavier (usually made of cast-iron) and deeper. A wok or deep-fat fryer makes a good substitute.

Other equipment: I find an electric spice grinder or an ordinary pestle and mortar are invaluable for grinding small quantities of spices. Food processors or electric blenders save many hours – and tears – when it comes to chopping up the mixture of onions, ginger and garlic which is often called for.

Cooking techniques

Because the sub-continent is so vast, methods of cooking differ from region to region. Let us start off with the preparation of spices.

Whole spices are often dry-roasted in a frying pan or fried in a small quantity of oil or ghee prior to being used whole, crushed or ground up for use in a recipe. They vary in thickness and hardness. Mustard seeds or fenugreek, for example, take longer than either cumin or coriander, so fry this type first and add the softer spices after them.

To dry-roast spices: Heat the pan until you can feel the heat if you hold your palm just above the surface. Add the hardest spices first, and stirring constantly, begin to cook them over medium heat. Once they start turning colour, add remaining spices and still stirring constantly, roast them all to an even brown. This is where your skill and judgement come into play: the spices should not be too light (still raw) nor too dark (burnt), but should have taken on just the right degree of colour. Practice will help you judge this. The spices are then removed from the pan and allowed to cool slightly before being crushed or ground for use in a recipe.

To fry spices: If a recipe calls for spices to be lightly fried, the same principle applies. The oil or ghee must always be fairly hot before the spices are added, or they will remain totally tasteless and become brittle. But if the fat is too hot the spices will burn before you have time to rescue them, and will ruin the dish. The important thing to remember is that the spices should sizzle, pop and splutter in the hot fat almost at once. The pan should then be taken off the heat and the spices removed at once to avoid the risk of burning. Always add the toughest spices and any dals that may be called for as flavourings first.

To grind or crush spices: You can use a coffee or spice mill, a pepper mill or a pestle and mortar. If you have none of these, place a sheet of greaseproof paper over the roasted spices and then crush them with a rolling pin. This will prevent them from sticking to the rolling pin, or making it smell.

Bhoona (frying): This is a very slow, gradual process in which a 'wet' mixture such as onions, ginger and garlic (or one or other of these) or a 'dry' mixture of spices, is gently fried (and constantly watched over and stirred) until it turns golden. It cannot be left or it will stick to the pan and burn.

It is important to keep stirring at this stage to prevent the ingredients from sticking to the bottom of the pan (you could also add a little water, if ground onions are used). Very soon, the vegetables will begin to release the oil or ghee that was absorbed during the initial frying. This is an indication that the mixture has reached the bhoona stage. Whole spices are now added and cooked until they release their flavour and aroma and finally, the main ingredient (meat, chicken, fish or vegetables) is added and stir-fried until it, too, loses its raw taste and takes on a glossy sheen.

Korma (braising): This technique is used in cooking all over the country and is especially important in non-vegetarian dishes. Meat and poultry is often first marinated in yogurt and spices, then cooked very slowly in the marinade.

Dum (pot roasting): The essential equipment for this ancient method of cooking meat, poultry or rice dishes is a heavy pan with a tight-fitting lid. Traditionally, once the ingredients have reached a stage where they can be left to cook, the lid is sealed to the pan with a dough paste which prevents any steam from escaping. The pan is then placed over high heat for a few minutes to build up enough steam inside, then the heat is reduced to low and the contents of the pan left to cook in their own juices. Traditionally, live charcoal or hot water is placed on the concave lid of the pan so food is effectively heated from the top and bottom. A delicious way of keeping in the flavour and aroma.

Tandoori cooking: An ancient method of cooking food which is still also in use today in the Middle and Far East. A tandoor is an unglazed clay oven heated by charcoal. Spiced, marinated meat, chicken, fish or other food is threaded on long metal skewers and then lowered into the blazing hot tandoor and left to bake. Nan, flat bread, is also slapped straight onto the hot side walls of the oven and bakes within a few minutes.

Marinating: Natural yogurt, lemon juice and ground, unripe green papaya (which contains papain, a natural enzyme which is widely used in commercial tenderising agents) are the main ingredients used for a marinade to tenderise meat, fish, poultry or game and also infuse the ingredients with the flavour and aroma of the spices.

Baghar: This is the final garnish or seasoning which is added to a dish (usually lentils) just before serving. Spices such as cumin, mustard, asafoetida, cloves, cardamoms, cinnamon, and chillies are usually used together with crisply fried onions, ginger and green chillies. These are quickly cooked in hot ghee (oil is not used because of its taste, nor butter, which burns easily).

Snacks and Starters

All over Pakistan people love eating snacks, whether out shopping or relaxing at home, and street vendors selling spicy tidbits are regular callers at the house. The daily ritual of eating snacks is part of the way of life where food is enjoyed along with the gossip. These snacks are so readily available from vendors that few are actually prepared in the home.

Every town and city has its own specialities, mingling the many influences of the sub-continent. Hot, spicy, crisp samosas are a favourite tea-time snack. The tuckshop at my school in Karachi sold the most unforgettable samosas I have ever eaten.

NARGISI KEBAB

Minced meat wrapped around hard-boiled eggs

Nargisi kebabs can be eaten as an appetizer if served with a chutney, or immersed into a rich sauce. It is important that the eggs are hard-boiled.

PREPARATION TIME: 15 MINUTES   COOKING TIME: 1 HOUR   SERVES: 4

450 g/1 lb lean mince (lamb or beef)
2 medium onions, skinned and cut into chunks
2–3 garlic cloves, skinned and cut into chunks
2.5 cm/1 inch piece fresh ginger, peeled and cut into chunks
1–2 green chillies, cut into large pieces
4–6 whole black peppercorns
4 cloves

2.5 cm/1 inch stick cinnamon
1 large black cardamom
75 g/3 oz channa dal, washed in a few changes of water
3.75 ml/¾ level tsp chilli powder
7.5 ml/1½ level tsp salt
6 hard boiled eggs, shelled
oil for frying

Thoroughly wash the mince and squeeze out any water (this is to get rid of any blood). Place all the ingredients except the egg and oil in a saucepan and pour in enough water to come about 4 cm (1/1½ inches) over the top. Cover and cook over low heat until the meat and dal are tender and all the moisture has dried up. (It is extremely important that all the water has dried up, otherwise the mince will not mould around the egg properly and will split open during frying.)

Place the mince in a blender or food processor or on a sill and grind it into a smooth paste. Take a lump of the mince paste and flatten it in the palm of your hand. Place a hard boiled egg in the middle of the mince and carefully mould this around the egg, taking care that no cracks appear on the surface. It is also important that the mince is tightly packed around the egg in order to prevent it from breaking off during frying.

Heat oil in a deep-fat fryer or karhai and carefully slip in 2 kebabs at a time. Fry to a rich golden colour, turning frequently to ensure even cooking. Serve hot.

PAKORAS

Gram flour fritters

Pakoras are a favourite tea-time snack all over Pakistan. They are quick and easy to make and consist of vegetables such as potatoes, onions, cauliflower, spinach, mushrooms, peppers, green chillies or other ingredients such as boiled eggs, paneer, chicken breast – which are coated in a spicy batter and then deep fried to a crisp golden colour.

PREPARATION TIME: 20 MINUTES   COOKING TIME: 15–20 MINUTES
SERVES: 4   ENOUGH TO COAT 450 g (1 lb) INGREDIENTS

Basic batter
100 g/4 oz gram flour, sieved (besan)
5 ml/1 level tsp salt
3.75 ml/¾ level tsp chilli powder
5 ml/1 level tsp ajowan seeds
5 ml/1 level tsp dried mint leaves (optional)

5 ml/1 level tsp garam masala (page 70)
about 150 ml/¼ pint water
450 g/1 lb prepared mixed vegetables such as potatoes, onions, cauliflower, mushrooms, aubergines, etc. or boiled eggs, paneer or chicken
oil for deep frying

Prepare the batter. Place the gram flour and the remaining dry ingredients in a bowl. Pour in the water gradually and beat to a smooth batter. The consistency should be like thick pancake batter. Leave aside to rest for 10 minutes. Meanwhile, prepare the vegetables:

Potatoes
Peel and slice into 1.25 cm (½ inch) thick slices. Soak in water until required to avoid discolouring. Drain and dry on absorbent kitchen paper before immersing in the batter.

Onions
Peel and slice into 1.25 cm (½ inch) thick round slices. Do not separate the layers.

Cauliflower
Cut into 5 cm (2 inch) long florets. If they are too thick, cut into half, otherwise they will remain uncooked.

Mushrooms
Peel if necessary. Wipe thoroughly.

Aubergines (baingan)
Slice into 1.25 cm (½ inch) thick round slices. Soak in acidulated cold water until required to avoid discolouration. Drain, dry and immerse in the batter.

Green chillies
For anyone who is feeling brave enough to tackle them. Make an incision on one side of the chilli lengthwise. This will stop them bursting during frying.

Eggs
Hard-boil the eggs. Shell and cut into slices or quarters.

Chicken
Use boned chicken breast. Cut into bite-size pieces. Marinate for 30 minutes in a little lemon juice, crushed garlic and green chilli. Drain and pat dry before use.

Once you have prepared the vegetables or other ingredients of your choice, lightly beat the batter for another minute or so.

Heat the oil in a deep-fat fryer or karhai to smoking point, then reduce the heat to medium. To test the temperature of the oil, sprinkle a few drops of batter into it, they should rise to the surface almost immediately. Remove them with a slotted slice and discard.

Dip a few pieces of the desired vegetables or other ingredients into the batter to thoroughly coat them, then using your fingers lift them out of the batter and at once drop them into the hot oil. Be careful not to splash yourself with the hot oil or let your fingers touch the hot oil by mistake. The safest way to avoid splashing is by gently lowering the fritter into the hot oil against the edge of the pan. Don't try to fry too many at a time. Fry for a few minutes, then carefully turn them over. They may tend to stick together, do not try to separate them now – this can be done after they have been taken out of the hot oil.

Fry the pakoras for 3–5 minutes to a crisp golden colour on both sides, drain thoroughly against the side of the pan with a perforated slice. Then place them on absorbent kitchen paper for a few minutes to absorb any excess oil. Serve hot.

SERVING SUGGESTION
Serve with Tamarind and Mint Chutney (page 60).

If you want to serve a large amount of pakoras, it is best to par-fry them in advance until the batter is cooked but not browned. Drain them and let them cool. Then re-fry as and when required until crisp and golden.

NAMKEEN DAL

Crunchy dal

A favourite snack for eating at any time. Whole or split washed moong dal, channa dal or whole Egyptian lentils are used for this spicy preparation. The pulses are first soaked in a mixture of milk and water and then deep fried. The cooked dal will keep well for several weeks.

PREPARATION TIME: 10 MINUTES PLUS OVERNIGHT SOAKING   COOKING TIME: 30 MINUTES

325 g/12 oz moong or channa dal
150 ml/¼ pint milk
1.4 litres/2½ pints water

oil for deep frying
7.5 ml/1½ level tsp salt
5 ml/1 level tsp chilli powder

Thoroughly wash the dals. In a large bowl mix together the milk and the water. Add the dal and leave it to soak overnight.

Next morning drain the dal and spread it out on a clean, dry cloth to dry off completely. Heat the oil to smoking point in a deep fat fryer or karhai. Sprinkle a handful of the dal into the hot oil and stand well back as it will splutter slightly. Fry for 2–3 minutes, then scoop it out with a perforated spoon. (Do not over-fry them or they will become hard and brittle.) Place them on absorbent kitchen paper to drain off any excess oil and allow to cool slightly. Sprinkle over the salt and chilli powder, mix thoroughly, then allow to cool completely. Store in airtight containers.

SERVING SUGGESTION
Excellent for serving with drinks such as Fresh Lime Drink (page 61).

KAYLE KE CHIPS

Banana chips

Finely-sliced, deep-fried green bananas make excellent crisps. Sprinkle some salt, chilli powder and dried mango powder on top, toss well and serve.

PREPARATION TIME: 20 MINUTES   COOKING TIME: 45 MINUTES   SERVES: 10–12

oil for deep frying
4 unripe green bananas
5 ml/1 level tsp salt

1.25 ml/¼ level tsp chilli powder
1.25 ml/¼ level tsp dried mango powder

Heat the oil in a deep-fat fryer or karhai. Peel the bananas and slice finely with a sharp knife. Although sticky, try to separate the slices as you drop them, a few at a time, into the hot oil. Turn them over once or twice, fry to a golden colour. Drain and spread them on absorbent kitchen paper to extract any excess oil.

When cold mix together the salt, chilli powder and mango powder, sprinkle on top and mix thoroughly. Serve with drinks or store in an airtight container until required.

SAMOSAS

Deep-fried pasties

I know of a small shop in Karachi which has a widespread reputation for preparing the best samosas in the city. Being a favourite tea-time snack, the long queues start building up long before the appointed time and it is not uncommon to wait for up to 20 minutes to obtain one of these delicious concoctions. Pastry is filled with a spicy mixture of mashed or finely sliced potatoes, shaped into a triangle, sealed and then deep-fried until rich and golden.

PREPARATION TIME: 25 MINUTES   COOKING TIME: 1 HOUR   MAKES: 60 SMALL SAMOSAS

Stuffing
450 g/1 lb potatoes
30 ml/2 tbsp vegetable oil
5 ml/1 level tsp cumin seeds
2 medium onions, skinned and finely chopped
2.5 cm/1 inch piece fresh ginger, peeled and finely
   chopped
2 green chillies, finely chopped
2.5 ml/½ level tsp chilli powder
5 ml/1 level tsp garam masala (page 70)
7.5 ml/1½ level tsp ground coriander

5 ml/1 level tsp dried mango powder
7.5 ml/1½ level tsp salt
a few sprigs fresh coriander leaves, finely chopped

Pastry
450 g/1 lb plain flour (maida)
5 ml/1 level tsp salt
15 ml/3 tbsp melted ghee or oil
about 200 ml/7 fl oz tepid water
oil for deep frying

Prepare the stuffing first as this has to cool down completely. Thoroughly scrub the potatoes free of any loose mud. Wash them, then boil them in their skins. Make sure that they do not split open during boiling. Drain and cool them sufficiently for ease of handling. Peel and finely chop.

Heat the oil in a large frying pan. Add the cumin seeds, and as soon as they pop and splutter add the finely chopped onions, ginger and green chillies. Stirring frequently, fry the mixture to a pale golden brown. Add the ground spices, mango powder and the salt. Stir-fry for another minute, then add the potatoes and the chopped coriander leaves. Stirring continuously, mix all the ingredients together and fry for about 5 minutes. Remove from heat and leave to cool down completely.

Meanwhile, prepare the pastry. Sift the flour and salt into a bowl. Pour in the melted ghee or oil and work it into the flour with your fingertips. The flour should resemble dry breadcrumbs. Pour in a little water at a time and bind the flour into a soft, pliable dough. Knead it really well for about 10 minutes. Cover with a piece of damp cloth and leave to rest for 15 minutes. Just before use, knead again for a few minutes.

Divide the dough into two equal halves. Roll each half into a long sausage shape with your hands, then break off or cut off 15 equal portions from each. Smear a little oil on to the palms of your hands then shape each portion into a perfect ball. At all times, keep the dough covered with a damp cloth to prevent a crust forming on top.

Smear a little oil onto a board or other rolling surface to prevent the dough from sticking. Roll out each ball into a round of 10 cm (4 inches) in diameter (or use a plain round cutter to obtain a neat even round) and virtually paper thin. Using a sharp knife cut into two halves.

Place one half on the palm of your hand and wet the edge with a little water. With the other hand, fold in one end towards the centre, taking care that the two layers don't stick together. Then fold the other edge over the first, so that it slightly overlaps and forms a cone.

Place 5 ml (1 tsp) of the cold stuffing into the hollow cone. Wet your fingers and lightly wet the top edges then press them together firmly so that they do not split open during frying. Prepare all the samosas and still keep them covered with a damp cloth.

Heat the oil in a deep fat-fryer or karhai. To test the temperature drop a small piece of pastry into it. It should float to the surface within a few seconds. Remove and discard the piece of pastry.

Carefully immerse 4 samosas into the hot oil at a time and fry over gentle heat, turning them over once or twice. Fry to a crisp golden colour (do not overbrown as that will harden the pastry). Drain against the sides of the pan and place on absorbent kitchen paper for a few minutes before serving hot.

SERVING SUGGESTION
Serve hot with Tamarind and Mint Chutney (page 60).

VARIATION
A spicy mince filling, using 450 g (1 lb) of mince can be used instead of potato. Cook the mince with the spices to an absolutely dry consistency then proceed as in the above recipe.

Fish and Shellfish

As Pakistan has a very small coastline, shellfish is not widely available. Karachi is the only seaport and does get a good supply of salt water fish and shell fish, but further inland they are rare. Although there are several large rivers in Pakistan, fresh water fish are only available seasonally. During the winter months melting snow from the high ground increases the flow of water and fishing, except for trout, is difficult. During the hot summer months the river beds dry up, and during the monsoon season the rivers are extremely muddy which makes the fish unsafe to eat.

However, there are some delicious dishes to be cooked with the fish available. Immigrants from Bangladesh, a predominately fish-eating area, have contributed many recipes to Pakistani cooking. Fish can be washed with a mixture of turmeric and besan (gram flour) to reduce the unpleasant fish smell.

PATRANI MACHCHI

Fish cooked in banana leaves

A classic Parsee dish that is absolutely out of this world. You can, of course, use foil instead of banana leaves if they are unavailable.

PREPARATION TIME: 15–20 MINUTES PLUS 30 MINUTES' MARINATING
COOKING TIME: 20–25 MINUTES   SERVES: 4

45 ml/3 tbsp lemon juice
5 ml/1 level tsp salt
700 g/1½ lb or 16 small pomfret (sole or plaice) fillets, skinned
5 ml/1 level tsp cumin seeds
10 ml/2 level tsp coriander seeds
5 ml/1 level tsp poppy seeds (khus khus)

1 garlic clove, skinned and crushed
2 green chillies, finely chopped
30 ml/2 level tbsp finely chopped fresh coriander leaves
60 ml/4 level tbsp fine desiccated coconut
60 ml/4 tbsp white distilled vinegar
10 ml/2 level tsp sugar
45 ml/3 tbsp vegetable oil

Mix the lemon juice and half the salt together and rub on both sides of each fillet. Leave to marinate for 30 minutes.

Meanwhile, prepare the rest of the ingredients. Dry roast the cumin and coriander seeds lightly and crush into a coarse powder while warm. In a bowl, mix the garlic, green chillies, crushed cumin and coriander, the poppy seeds, chopped fresh coriander, desiccated coconut, remaining salt, the vinegar and the sugar.

Divide the fillets between 4 pieces of foil. Coat liberally on both sides with the coconut mixture. Brush all over with a little oil. Fold over foil and seal the edges. Place foil envelopes on a flat baking tray and bake at 190°C (375°F) mark 5 for 20–25 minutes.

MACHCHI KA SADA SALAN

Fish in a simple sauce

Karachi being the seaport of Pakistan, fish is always available. Any large fish is suitable for this recipe.

PREPARATION TIME: 20 MINUTES   COOKING TIME: 20 MINUTES   SERVES: 4

4.4 cm/1¾ inch thick white fish steaks, washed and
    dried
2–3 garlic cloves, skinned
2.5 cm/1 inch piece fresh ginger, peeled
2 green chillies
2.5 ml/½ level tsp chilli powder

2.5 ml/½ level tsp turmeric
5 ml/1 level tsp salt
45 ml/3 tbsp oil
3 medium onions, skinned and finely chopped
150 ml/¼ pint water
15 ml/1 tbsp freshly chopped coriander leaves

Wash and thoroughly dry the fish steaks. In a blender or food processor grind the garlic, ginger and chillies to a fine paste. Smear the fish with the spice paste, chilli powder, turmeric and salt. Set aside for at least 20 minutes.

In the meantime heat the oil in a shallow frying pan, add the chopped onions and, stirring frequently, fry them to a rich golden colour. Add the marinated fish and, turning carefully once or twice, cook until the oil begins to sizzle once more. Add the water, cover with a tight fitting lid, reduce the heat and cook for 10–15 minutes until the steaks are tender and they still retain their shape. The excess water should have dried up by this time. Sprinkle with coriander leaves and serve hot.

TANDOORI MACHCHI

Tandoori fish

The special aroma of this dish is derived from the tandoor, the traditional unglazed clay oven which is heated with charcoal. Punjabis favour fish cooked dry rather than in a sauce and so this recipe calls for marinated fish to be roasted in the oven. Where a tandoor is not available, it can be barbecued, though you can cook it under a hot grill or in a fish brick.

PREPARATION TIME: 5–10 MINUTES PLUS 3 HOURS' MARINATING   COOKING TIME: 20 MINUTES
SERVES: 4

4 small pomfret (sole or plaice) cleaned but with heads
    and tails on
5 cm/2 inch piece fresh ginger, peeled and coarsely
    chopped
2 garlic cloves, skinned
1 green chilli
5 ml/1 level tsp ground cumin

1.25 ml/¼ level tsp ground turmeric
1.25 ml/¼ level tsp chilli powder
7.5 ml/1½ level tsp sweet paprika (deghi mirch)
60 ml/4 tbsp lemon juice
5 ml/1 level tsp salt
5 ml/1 level tsp garam masala (page 70)
30 ml/2 tbsp vegetable oil

Wash the fish thoroughly inside and out; pat dry. Slash in 3–4 places on both sides. Put chopped ginger, garlic and chilli in a blender or food processor and blend the mixture to a smooth paste.

Add the remaining ingredients except the oil and stir well. Place fish in a large flat dish, and pour this marinade over, rubbing it well into the cuts on both sides. Cover and leave to marinate for 3 hours.

Prepare the barbecue. The burning charcoal should be covered with white ash before you begin to cook the fish.

Pierce each fish with a large skewer for ease of turning. Brush on both sides with some oil and barbecue (or grill or bake) for about 20 minutes or until the skin is well browned and crisp.

Turn the fish once during cooking and keep brushing with oil to prevent burning.

SOOKHA JHINGHA

Spicy dry prawns

A quick and easy dish to prepare. Large prawns are best for this dish, but do thaw them out completely if frozen ones are used.

PREPARATION TIME: 15 MINUTES   COOKING TIME: 15 MINUTES   SERVES: 4

8 king-sized prawns, thawed and peeled
2 bunches spring onions
15 ml/1 level tbsp light sesame oil (til ka tail)
2.5 ml/½ level tsp cumin seeds
1.25 ml/¼ level tsp chilli powder

1.25 ml/¼ level tsp ground turmeric
3.75 ml/¾ level tsp salt
30 ml/2 level tbsp finely chopped fresh coriander leaves
    (optional)

Drain the prawns and squeeze gently to remove any excess water. Cut any limp green leaves off the onions and remove the roots. Chop into 1.25 cm (½ inch) pieces.

Heat the oil in a saucepan, add the cumin seeds, and as soon as they pop, add the chopped onions and the chilli powder, turmeric and salt. Stirring frequently, fry for 2–3 minutes to a pale golden colour. Add the prawns and continue stirring and frying until all the moisture dries up and the prawns are tender. Garnish with coriander and serve at once.

CHINGHRI JHAL

Bengali-style baked prawns

A truly delicious dish of king-sized prawns, cooked in the oven with coconut and spices. Use the largest prawns you can find, and afford.

PREPARATION TIME: 25 MINUTES   COOKING TIME: 35 MINUTES   SERVES: 4

450 g/1 lb king-sized prawns, uncooked
2.5 cm/1 inch piece fresh ginger, peeled
1 garlic clove, skinned
2 green chillies, seeded
60 ml/4 level tbsp desiccated coconut
15 ml/1 level tbsp white mustard seeds
2.5 ml/½ level tsp ground turmeric

2.5 ml/½ level tsp salt
5 ml/1 level tsp sugar
30 ml/2 tbsp mustard oil
5 ml/1 tsp panch foran (page 70)
5 ml/1 level tbsp finely chopped fresh coriander leaves
lemon wedges and onion rings

Shell the prawns, remove the heads; devein the prawns. (If using frozen prawns, thaw completely and squeeze out any excess water.) In a blender or food processor grind the ginger, garlic, chillies into a smooth paste and mix this with the desiccated coconut, mustard seeds, turmeric, salt and the sugar.

Pour the mustard oil into a small frying pan and heat to smoking point to get rid of the pungent taste and smell. Add the panch foran and as soon as the seeds pop and splutter, pour the contents of the pan over the ground ingredients. Put the prawns in a large, ovenproof dish and coat them liberally with the mixture. Cover with a lid or foil and bake at 190°C (375°F) mark 5 for about 25–30 minutes until cooked. Remove from the oven, garnish with chopped fresh coriander, lemon wedges and onion rings and serve hot.

MACHCHLI KE SEEKH KEBABS

Barbecued fish seekh kebabs

These are delicious when barbecued, but can be grilled indoors quite successfully. The onion is first fried to a crisp golden colour, then ground and added to the marinade. This adds a totally different flavour and aroma to the fish.

PREPARATION TIME: 20 MINUTES PLUS 5 HOURS' MARINATING   COOKING TIME: 15 MINUTES
SERVES: 4

450 g/1 lb cod (white fish) fillets, skinned
30 ml/2 tbsp natural yogurt
2 medium onions, skinned; one coarsely chopped, one finely sliced
1 garlic clove, skinned and chopped
2.5 cm/1 inch piece fresh ginger, peeled and chopped

1 green chilli
2.5 ml/$\frac{1}{2}$ level tsp black cumin seeds
5 ml/1 level tsp salt
5 ml/1 level tsp garam masala (page 70)
30 ml/2 tbsp vegetable oil
lemon wedges, onion rings for garnish

Cut the cod fillets into 2.5 cm/ 1 inch cubes. Place yogurt in a bowl. In a blender or food processor blend one chopped onion, the garlic, ginger, green chilli, black cumin seeds, salt and garam masala to a fine paste. Add to the yogurt and mix well. Add the fish to this paste and mix well. Cover and marinate for 4 hours.

Heat 15 ml (1 tbsp) of the oil in a small frying pan and stirring frequently, fry the sliced onion for 10 minutes to a rich golden colour. Grind this onion to a paste and add to the yogurt marinade. Mix well and leave to marinate for a further 1 hour.

Meanwhile prepare the barbecue and when the coals are covered by white ash, thread fish pieces on long skewers. Brush with oil and cook for 10–15 minutes, turning frequently to brown evenly. Alternatively, cook under a hot grill. Remove from skewers and serve at once. Garnish with lemon wedges and onion rings.

KASHMIRI MACHCHI

Fish Kashmir-style

During my short but memorable stay in Murree I tasted this dish at a small café. The delicate spicing of aniseeds enhances the taste of the fish.

PREPARATION TIME: 10 MINUTES   COOKING TIME: 35 MINUTES   SERVES: 4

4 trout, each weighing about 225 g (8 oz) cleaned
30 ml/2 tbsp mustard oil
1.25 ml/$\frac{1}{4}$ level tsp asafoetida (hing)
30 ml/2 level tbsp aniseed, finely crushed (sauf)
5 ml/1 level tsp ginger powder

3.75 ml/$\frac{3}{4}$ level tsp chilli powder
5 ml/1 level tsp salt
2.5 ml/$\frac{1}{2}$ level tsp ground turmeric
90 ml/6 tbsp natural yogurt, lightly whipped
450 g/1 lb medium turnips, peeled and cut into 1 cm/$\frac{1}{2}$ inch cubes

Remove the head and tail and cut trout into 2.5 cm (1 inch) thick steaks. Heat the mustard oil to smoking point to remove the pungent taste and smell.

In a large, heavy-based frying pan, add the asafoetida and follow at once with the aniseed, ginger powder, chilli powder, salt and the turmeric. Stir-fry for a minute, then gradually add the yogurt, 15 ml (1 tbsp) at a time. Stirring continuously, mix well and fry each small batch of yogurt until the oil begins to separate.

Add the turnips. Mix well and place the fish steaks on top. Try not to overlap them. Spoon the yogurt mixture over them. Cover with a tight-fitting lid, reduce the heat and cook for 25–30 minutes until the turnips and the fish are tender and the sauce has thickened. Serve at once.

MASALA ROHU

White fish in a tomato sauce

This recipe was given to me by an old gentleman who used to cook for the royal household of Jaipur and who, during Partition, moved to Lahore. Rohu is a feshwater fish with a very delicate flavour; I find that cod makes a good substitute.

PREPARATION TIME: 30 MINUTES   COOKING TIME: 35–40 MINUTES   SERVES: 4

450 g/1 lb cod or any other firm white fish fillets
30 ml/2 tbsp vegetable oil
5 ml/1 level tsp cumin seeds
2.5 ml/½ level tsp mustard seeds
2 medium onions, skinned and finely chopped
1 garlic clove, skinned and finely chopped
2.5 cm/1 inch piece fresh ginger, peeled and finely chopped

1 green chilli, finely chopped
2.5 ml/½ level tsp ground turmeric
1.25 ml/¼ level tsp chilli powder
2.5 ml/½ level tsp garam masala (page 70)
5 ml/1 level tsp salt
3 ripe tomatoes, skinned and finely chopped
150 ml/¼ pint water
30 ml/2 level tbsp finely chopped fresh coriander leaves

Wash the fish and pat dry. Cut into 2.5 cm (1 inch) pieces. Heat the oil in a large, shallow heavy-based saucepan and add the cumin and mustard seeds; they should pop and splutter at once. Add the finely chopped onions, garlic, ginger, and green chilli. Stirring frequently, fry for 10–15 minutes until the onions are a rich golden colour. Add the turmeric, chilli powder, garam masala and the salt. Stirring, fry for another minute then add the chopped tomatoes. Still stirring frequently, fry the onion mixture for about 10 minutes until the tomatoes are reduced to a pulp. Add a little water, if necessary, to prevent the mixture from sticking to the bottom of the pan. Keep frying until the oil begins to separate.

Add the fish and stir well to coat it with the tomato mixture. Reduce the heat to low, cover with a tight fitting lid and cook for 15 minutes until the fish is tender. Serve hot, sprinkled with finely chopped coriander.

MACHCHER JHAL

Fish in mustard sauce

Bengali cuisine is noted for its use of mustard oil and mustard seed which impart a unique flavour and aroma to the food.

PREPARATION TIME: 25 MINUTES   COOKING TIME: 35–40 MINUTES   SERVES: 4–6

700 g/1½ lb cod or any firm white fish
mustard oil for deep frying
2.5 cm/1 inch piece fresh ginger, peeled and roughly chopped
1 green chilli, roughly chopped
3.75 ml/¾ level tsp ground turmeric

30 ml/2 level tbsp brown mustard seeds
600 ml/1 pint water
5 ml/1 tsp panch foran (page 70)
2.5 ml/½ level tsp salt
30 ml/2 level tbsp finely chopped fresh coriander leaves

Wash the fish and pat dry. Cut into 5 cm (2 inch) pieces. Heat the mustard oil to smoking point in a deep frying pan to remove the pungent smell and taste. Add a few pieces of fish at a time and fry for 10 minutes to a crisp golden brown. Drain and keep aside.

Place the ginger, chilli, turmeric, mustard seeds and 60 ml (4 tbsp) of the water in a food processor and mix to a fine, smooth paste. Add the remaining water and mix thoroughly. Stand for 5 minutes, stir, then pass through a fine sieve. Reserve the liquid and discard any pulp in the strainer.

In a saucepan heat 30 ml (2 tbsp) of mustard oil to smoking point. Add the panch foran. As soon as the seeds begin to pop and splutter, stand well back and add the mustard flavoured liquid and the salt. Increase the heat and boil rapidly, stirring, until the liquid is reduced by half. Reduce the heat to let the sauce simmer down. Add the fried fish and let it simmer for another 5 minutes (no longer or it will disintegrate). Transfer to a heated dish. Sprinkle with chopped coriander and serve at once.

SAS NI MACHCHI

Parsee-style fish

Parsee cuisine is distinctive in its use of ingredients. This recipe makes a clever use of eggs and vinegar to create a sauce for fish. Pomfret is the traditional choice of fish for this dish, but you can use sole or plaice instead.

PREPARATION TIME: 35 MINUTES   COOKING TIME: 45–50 MINUTES   SERVES: 4

1 large pomfret or sole or plaice, about 700 g/1½ lb, filleted
4 small dried red chillies, chopped
2 small garlic cloves, skinned and chopped
5 ml/1 level tsp cumin seeds
300 ml/½ pint water
30 ml/2 level tbsp ghee
2 medium onions, skinned and finely sliced

3 ripe tomatoes, roughly chopped
a few sprigs fresh coriander leaves, roughly chopped
5 ml/1 level tsp salt
2 eggs
45 ml/2 tbsp white distilled vinegar
10 ml/2 tsp plain flour (maida)
5 ml/1 level tsp sugar
2.5 ml/½ level tsp black peppercorns, lightly crushed

Wash the fish and pat dry. Cut into 2.5 cm (1 inch) thick slices. In a blender or food processor, grind the chopped chillies, garlic and cumin seeds to a smooth paste (you may need to add a little water to help the process).

Heat the ghee in a suaté pan and add the sliced onions. Stirring frequently, fry for 5–10 minutes to an even golden brown. Add the ground garlic mixture and continue frying for another few minutes. Then add the chopped tomatoes and coriander leaves. Stirring frequently, fry the mixture until the tomatoes are reduced to a pulp and the ghee begins to separate, about 10 minutes. If the mixture sticks to the bottom add 15 ml (1 tbsp) water at a time and continue frying.

Add the remaining water and mix well. Bring to the boil, then reduce the heat and cook for about 5 minutes. Add the fish and the salt. Cover with a tight-fitting lid and continue cooking for 10–15 minutes until the fish is tender. Remove from heat and leave to cool slightly.

Meanwhile, in a bowl, lightly whip the eggs, vinegar, plain flour and the sugar. When the fish has cooled down and no more steam is rising, add the egg mixture and the crushed pepper; then turn the fish over to cover completely in the mixture. Over low heat, simmer gently for 5–8 minutes until the egg mixture begins to thicken. Care must be taken not to let the mixture bubble as that may curdle the egg. Remove from heat and serve.

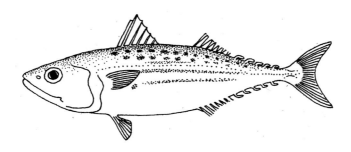

Meat

Although Pakistanis love eating rich foods cooked in plenty of ghee (clarified butter), they are not fond of eating animal fat and will not cook with it either. Meat sold in Pakistan, therefore, is trimmed of any extra fat and then weighed before being sold to the customer. The only time that meat with a little fat is used is in the preparation of dishes such as a pullao or a biriyani, in which the fat acts to keep the rice soft and moist.

Meat is often marinated in Pakistani cooking, not only to improve its flavour but also to tenderise it. Ingredients such as lemon juice or yogurt are mixed with spices and the meat is left to steep in the mixture for a set period of time. Fresh, unripe papaya (paw paw) is another natural ingredient that is used to tenderise meat (papain, the enzyme from papaya, is included in powdered tenderisers available over here). Fortunately, no artificial meat tenderisers are yet used in Pakistani homes.

Cooking methods

Meat cooked in Pakistan is always fried using the bhoona method, in which it is stir-fried over medium heat in a mixture of ghee or oil and spices for about 20 minutes until it becomes a rich, brown colour, no longer tastes raw and begins to release the fat in which it was cooked. By the time the meat reaches this bhoona stage, it is almost tender. Only a little liquid needs to be added if a sauce is called for and very little cooking is required to finish the dish. Bhoona is an excellent method for cooking cheaper cuts of meat. Plain water is the usual liquid added to make a sauce, though meat bones are used to make rich stocks for use in special dishes such as biriyanis.

Another popular way of cooking meat is by the dum method, in which the lid of the cooking pan is sealed with a paste of dough (page 71). Live charcoal is then put on the lid and the sealed pan placed over a flame. The heat then reaches the pan from above and below and recreates the effect of an oven and steam trapped inside helps to cook the meat.

In Pakistan, many dishes are cooked over an open fire, for apart from the tandoor, the traditional clay oven, no other sort of oven exists and modern gas and electric stoves are just finding their place in the market. Tandoori food is a speciality of the Punjab and the Northwest. Only lean meat can be cooked this way for the heat is fierce. Tough cuts of meat require long, slow cooking and would never have time to become tender in the short time it takes to cook the outside. When making a 'tandoori' dish in a western kitchen, marinate it first and then, for best results, cook the meat on a barbecue over charcoal; conventional ovens can, of course, be used as well if a barbecue is not practical.

Many different types of kebabs are made from meat. One worth mentioning – and there is no recipe for it in this book for reasons which will become obvious – is Pathar ke kebab, which when translated means 'kebabs of stone'. Thin slices of lamb, cut from the leg, are first marinated in spices and unripe papaya. A slab of marble about 5–7 cm (2–3 inches) thick is then placed on top of an open charcoal fire and allowed to become really hot – this takes anything from 30–45 minutes. The meat is placed on top of the hot marble and within a few minutes is cooked to perfection. The kebabs are eaten as a starter with mint and yogurt chutney. Delicious! Minced meat is also used in a variety of kebab dishes. It is ground to a very fine paste. This means putting it through the mincer at least twice, or processing it very well in a blender or food processor and when cooked it just melts in the mouth.

The recipes in this chapter range from very basic dishes to elaborate ones. There is no equivalent concept of 'meat and two veg' in Pakistani meals, and often meat and vegetables are cooked together.

Shami kebabs and Seekh kebabs

GOSHT AUR PHOOLGOBI KA SALAN

Meat with cauliflower

Various vegetables can be combined with meat to create a range of dishes. In this recipe I have used cauliflower with meat. An excellent dish for lunch as it is not overwhelmingly rich.

PREPARATION TIME: 20 MINUTES PLUS 30 MINUTES STANDING COOKING TIME: 1 HOUR
SERVES: 4

450 g/1 lb lean boneless lamb
1.25 cm/½ inch piece fresh ginger
2 garlic cloves, skinned
2 green chillies
2.5 ml/½ level tsp chilli powder
2.5 ml/½ level tsp turmeric
7.5 ml/½ level tsp salt

1 small cauliflower
30 ml/2 tbsp oil or ghee
3 medium onions, skinned and finely chopped
300 ml/½ pint water
15 ml/1 level tbsp finely chopped coriander leaves
lemon wedges

Trim excess fat from the meat and cut into 2.5 cm (1 inch) pieces. Thoroughly wash and dry the meat. In a blender or food processor grind the ginger, garlic, green chilli, chilli powder, turmeric and the salt to a fine paste. Rub it all over the meat. Cover and let it stand for at least 30 minutes.

Meanwhile, prepare the cauliflower. Remove any of the coarser stalks. Break the rest of the cauliflower into medium-sized florets.

Heat the oil in a heavy-based saucepan. Add the cauliflower and fry to a pale golden colour. Strain and set aside. To the hot ghee, add the chopped onions and fry to a pale golden brown. Add the meat and the spices and stirring frequently, fry the meat to a light brown colour. Add the water, mix well, then cover and cook over low heat until the meat is tender. Remember to stir it from time to time to prevent it from sticking.

Add the fried cauliflower and carefully mix it in. Try not to break up the florets. Cover and cook for another 5 minutes until the florets have absorbed some of the flavour.

Sprinkle with the coriander leaves and serve hot. Decorate with lemon wedges.

KEEMA MATTAR

Spicy mince with peas

An all time favourite where each household has its own additions to the basic ingredients.

PREPARATION TIME: 25 MINUTES   COOKING TIME: 50 MINUTES   SERVES: 4

450 g/1 lb lean minced lamb or beef
100 g/4 oz canned tomatoes, with the juice
2 medium onions, skinned and finely chopped
2 garlic cloves, skinned and finely chopped
2.5 cm/1 inch piece fresh ginger, peeled and finely chopped
2.5 ml/½ level tsp chilli powder
2.5 ml/½ level tsp ground turmeric

10 ml/2 level tsp ground coriander
5 ml/1 level tsp ground cumin
2.5 ml/½ level tsp garam masala (page 70)
5 ml/1 level tsp dried mint leaves
6.25 ml/1¼ level tsp salt
225 g/8 oz frozen or fresh peas
150 ml/¼ pint natural yogurt (dahi)
30 ml/2 tbsp lemon juice

Put the mince in a heavy-based saucepan over low heat and, stirring occasionally, let the mince cook in its own fat until all the moisture evaporates. Chop the tomatoes.

Add the chopped onion, garlic, ginger, the powdered spices, dried mint, salt, tomatoes and peas. Mix them all well, cover and leave to cook over low heat for 45–50 minutes until the ingredients are well blended and the mince and peas are tender. The natural fat from the mince will begin to separate.

Pour in the yogurt and lemon juice. Stirring constantly, fry the mince until the yogurt and the juice are well absorbed. Transfer to a heated serving dish and serve piping hot.

Kashmiri raan

BHOOJELO GOSHT

Parsee barbecued lamb

Yogurt and lemon juice are commonly used as meat tenderisers. Fresh papaya, or paw paw, is widely used in many parts of the world for the same purpose but this property of the fruit is little known in the West, though it is a constituent of many proprietary brands of powdered tenderiser. This recipe for barbecued mutton is given added tang by the use of Worcestershire sauce. You can always grill the meat conventionally if you do not have a charcoal grill.

PREPARATION TIME: 20 MINUTES PLUS 10 HOURS' OR OVERNIGHT MARINATING
COOKING TIME: 15 MINUTES   SERVES: 4

450 g/1 lb boned tender lamb
1 garlic clove, skinned and chopped
2.5 cm/1 inch piece fresh ginger, peeled and chopped
7.5 ml/1½ level tsp cumin seeds
4 whole black peppercorns
30 ml/2 level tbsp coriander seeds
5 ml/1 level tsp chilli powder

5 ml/1 level tsp sugar
5 ml/1 level tsp salt
50 g/2 oz raw papaya, peeled and chopped
30 ml/2 tbsp vinegar
15 ml/1 tbsp Worcestershire sauce
45 ml/3 tbsp vegetable oil

Trim any excess fat from the meat. Cut into 2.5 cm (1 inch) cubes and keep aside in a bowl. In a blender or food processor, blend the chopped garlic, ginger, cumin seeds, black peppercorns, coriander seeds, chilli powder, sugar, salt and papaya to a smooth paste.

Add the vinegar and grind for another minute. Then add the Worcestershire sauce and the oil and mix all the ingredients. Add the ground mixture to the meat and coat thoroughly. Cover and place in refrigerator to marinate for 10 hours. Stir from time to time.

Prepare the barbecue or heat the grill. Thread a few pieces of meat on to each skewer and cook, turning frequently, for about 15 minutes, until the lamb is tender and well browned. Remove from the skewers and serve without delay.

KOTMIR KA SALAN

Lamb with fragrant coriander leaves

Fresh coriander provides the predominant flavour in this succulent lamb dish.

PREPARATION TIME: 30 MINUTES   COOKING TIME: 2 HOURS   SERVES: 4

450 g/1 lb boned tender lamb cut into small pieces
2 garlic cloves, skinned and coarsely chopped
2.5 cm/1 inch piece fresh ginger, peeled and coarsely chopped
125 g/5 oz coarsely chopped fresh coriander leaves

3 green chillies, coarsley chopped
45 ml/3 level tbsp ghee
4 medium onions, skinned and finely chopped
2.5 ml/½ level tsp ground turmeric
5 ml/1 level tsp salt

Trim any excess fat from the meat. Put chopped garlic and ginger in a blender or food processor and blend to a fine paste; reserve. Repeat with the coriander and green chillies. Rub the ginger and garlic paste thoroughly into the meat. Heat the ghee in a heavy saucepan, add the chopped onions and, stirring frequently, fry the mixture for 5 to 10 minutes to a crisp golden colour.

Add the meat, turmeric and the salt. Stirring frequently, fry for a few minutes. Reduce the heat to its lowest setting, cover with a tight fitting lid and cook for 1¼ hours or until the meat is almost tender. Add the coriander and chilli paste. Stir well to mix all the ingredients. Continue cooking for another 30 minutes until all the moisture has dried up. Serve at once.

GOSHT DO-PIAZA

Meat Do-Piaza

Opinions vary on the meaning of the term Do-Piaza. Taken literally it means 'two onions', but the dish was named originally after a minister of the Emperor Akbar, Mullah Do-Piaza. In the context of cooking techniques, this term is often interpreted to mean using twice the weight of onions to meat.

PREPARATION TIME: 30 MINUTES   COOKING TIME: 1¼–1¾ HOURS   SERVES: 4

450 g/1 lb boned tender lamb or beef
vegetable oil
1 kg/2¼ lb onions, skinned; 2 finely sliced, the rest finely chopped
10 ml/2 level tsp ground coriander
5 ml/1 level tsp chilli powder
1.25 ml/¼ level tsp ground turmeric
5 ml/1 level tsp salt

45 ml/3 tbsp vegetable oil
2 garlic cloves, skinned and crushed
2.5 cm/1 inch piece fresh ginger, peeled and finely sliced
2 bay leaves, crushed
4 ripe tomatoes, skinned and roughly chopped
30 ml/2 tbsp lemon juice
30 ml/2 level tbsp finely chopped fresh coriander leaves

Trim any excess fat from the meat; cut into 4 cm (1½ inch) pieces. Lightly grease a heavy-based saucepan with a dash of vegetable oil. Spread half the chopped onions on the bottom. Add the meat and sprinkle with ground coriander, chilli powder, turmeric and salt and layer the rest of the chopped onions on top. Cover pan with a tight fitting lid and cook gently for about 1¼ hours until the onions are reduced to a pulp and the meat is tender.

Meanwhile, heat the oil in another pan. Add the 2 sliced onions, the crushed garlic and the finely sliced ginger. Stirring frequently, fry for about 10 minutes to a rich golden colour.

Add the crushed bay leaves and stir-fry for another few minutes. Add the chopped tomatoes and continue frying, stirring frequently, until the tomatoes are reduced to a pulp. Add the contents of the other pan – the meat and the onions. Stir well to mix all the ingredients. Stirring frequently, fry the mixture until it is well browned and has formed a thick onion sauce. Add the lemon juice. Fry for another few minutes, mixing well. Transfer to a heated dish, sprinkle with chopped coriander and serve.

SHAMI KEBABS

Kebabs are associated largely with various countries of the Middle East, but they are popular in Pakistan as well. This recipe is peculiar to Lucknow in India – and makes mouthwatering kebabs. The channa dal is boiled with the mince and spices and acts as a binder, adding its own, musky flavour.

PREPARATION TIME: 30 MINUTES PLUS 2 HOURS' SOAKING AND 30 MINUTES' CHILLING
COOKING TIME: 1½ HOURS   SERVES: 4–6 (MAKES ABOUT 24)

100 g/4 oz channa dal
450 g/1 lb lean lamb or beef mince
1 medium onion, skinned and roughly chopped
2 garlic cloves, skinned and roughly chopped
2.5 cm/1 inch piece fresh ginger, peeled and roughly
  chopped
2 black cardamoms, seeded
10 whole black peppercorns
5 ml/1 level tsp cumin seeds
2 whole dried red chillies

5 ml/1 level tsp salt
300 ml/½ pint water
1 egg, beaten

Stuffing
1 medium onion, peeled and finely chopped
2 level tbsp finely chopped fresh coriander leaves
2 green chillies, finely chopped
oil for shallow frying

Put the dal in a sieve and wash thoroughly until the water runs clear. Soak in plenty of water for 2 hours. Drain and put in a large saucepan. Add the mince, chopped onion, garlic, ginger, black cardamom seeds, peppercorns, cumin seeds, red chillies, salt and water to the dal.

Simmer briskly, uncovered, for 45 minutes until the meat is tender and the water has been completely absorbed (this is very important, otherwise the kebabs will split on frying). Remove from heat and allow to become cool enough to handle. Put the mince in a food processor or blender, add the beaten egg and grind to a very smooth, thick paste which holds its shape.

Prepare the stuffing. Mix together the chopped onion, coriander leaves and green chillies. Break off 15 ml (1 tbsp) of the mince paste. Wet your palms and place it in the centre of your palm. Shape it into a smooth ball (keep wetting your hands to prevent the paste from sticking to your palms). Indent the centre with your thumb and press a little of the stuffing mixture into it. Fold the sides over carefully and reshape into a smooth, flat shape. Repeat with remaining mince. Chill in the refrigerator for 30 minutes.

Heat a heavy-based frying pan and add just enough oil to just cover the surface (if there is too much oil the kebabs will split). Add 3–4 kebabs at a time and fry over a very low heat to a crisp golden colour, turning them once. Keep hot while you fry the remaining kebabs. Remove from frying pan carefully and serve.

SEEKH KEBABS

In this recipe, kebabs on a skewer are grilled over live charcoal or under a grill. This is one of the few Pakistani dishes in which allspice has been used.

PREPARATION TIME: 20–25 MINUTES   COOKING TIME: 30 MINUTES   SERVES: 4

2.5 ml/½ level tsp allspice (kebab chini)
25 g/1 oz poppy seeds (khus khus)
25 g/1 oz chirongi nuts (page 76) or blanched
  almonds
1.25 cm/½ inch, piece fresh ginger, peeled
1 garlic clove, skinned
15 ml/1 level tbsp finely chopped fresh coriander leaves

25 g/1 oz unripe green papaya
450 g/1 lb lean minced lamb or beef
2.5 ml/½ level tsp chilli powder
5 ml/1 level tsp salt
50 g/2 oz roasted chick pea flour
30 ml/2 tbsp melted ghee
30 ml/2 tbsp lemon juice

Dry-roast the allspice, poppy seeds and the nuts for a few minutes in a small heavy-based frying pan until they give off their aroma. Put in a blender or food processor with the ginger, garlic, coriander and papaya and blend to a paste.

Put the mince and the paste in a bowl. Add the chilli powder and the salt. Knead the mixture really well for a few minutes with your hands until the mince holds its shape and is soft and pliable (or put in a blender or food processor and grind to a smooth paste).

Sieve in the roasted chick pea flour. Knead the mince again until it feels completely dry to the touch (add a little extra flour if needed). Mix together the melted ghee and lemon juice in a separate bowl.

Break off large pieces of the mince and mould them into kebabs on long skewers. Brush the kebabs with the melted ghee mixture. Put skewers carefully over a gentle charcoal flame or under a grill. Cook for 5 minutes until pale brown on each side, basting frequently and turning a few times. Remove from skewers and serve at once.

LUCKNOWI KORMA

Lamb korma

This is an everyday korma in many homes and the spicing is kept to the minimum. On festive occasions, a richer dish is made in which case as many as 20 spices are used to create a truly rich and delicious meal.

PREPARATION TIME: 40 MINUTES   COOKING TIME: ABOUT 2 HOURS   SERVES: 4

450 g/1 lb boned tender lamb
60 ml/4 tbsp natural yogurt (dahi)
3 large onions, skinned and coarsely chopped
2 garlic cloves, skinned and chopped
2.5 cm/1 inch piece fresh ginger, peeled and chopped
45 ml/3 level tbsp ghee
8 black peppercorns, coarsely crushed
4 green cardamoms, coarsely crushed

1 black cardamom, coarsley crushed
2 cloves, coarsely crushed
5 ml/1 level tsp salt
5 ml/1 level tsp chilli powder
10 ml/2 level tsp ground coriander
600 ml/1 pint water
15 ml/1 level tbsp chopped fresh coriander leaves

Remove all excess fat from the meat. Cut into 4 cm (1½ inch) pieces. Spoon the yogurt into a piece of muslin draped over a bowl; tie up ends securely and hang to drain over the bowl.

Keep one chopped onion aside. Put the remaining onions, garlic and ginger in a blender or food processor and blend to a smooth paste.

Heat the ghee in a heavy-based saucepan, add the roughly chopped onion and, stirring frequently, fry to a pale golden colour. Add the crushed spices, salt and meat. Stirring constantly, fry the meat for 5–8 minutes to a rich brown colour. The ghee will start to separate at this stage. Add the ground onion paste. Continue stirring and frying for another 10 minutes until the mixture is well browned. Add the chilli powder and the ground coriander. Stir well, then add the drained yogurt 15 ml (1 tbsp) at a time and, stirring continuously, fry until the ghee once again begins to separate.

Soon after this the masala will begin to stick to the bottom of the pan. This is an indication that the meat has been cooked enough and you can now add the water. Mix well. Cover with a tight fitting lid, reduce the heat and simmer for 1¼ to 1½ hours or until the meat is really tender and the sauce has thickened.

Transfer to a heated dish, sprinkle with coriander leaves and serve hot.

SAG GOSHT

Meat cooked with spinach

The spinach for this recipe can be fresh or frozen and in either leaf or purée form. To keep the fat content down, I first marinate the meat in yogurt and spices, then add the spinach and a hint of ghee towards the end.

PREPARATION TIME: 30 MINUTES PLUS 4 HOURS' MARINATING
COOKING TIME: 1¼ HOURS   SERVES: 4

450 g/1 lb boned tender lamb or beef
90 ml/6 tbsp natural yogurt
2.5 cm/1 inch piece fresh ginger, peeled
2 garlic cloves, skinned
2.5 cm/1 inch stick cinnamon
2 bay leaves
4 green cardamoms
8 black peppercorns
6 cloves

5 ml/1 level tsp cumin seeds
5 ml/1 level tsp garam masala (page 70)
2.5 ml/½ level tsp chilli powder
7.5 ml/1½ level tsp ground coriander
5 ml/1 level tsp salt
450 g/1 lb fresh or 225 g/8 oz frozen spinach
45 ml/3 level tbsp ghee
1 medium onion, skinned and finely sliced

Remove any excess fat from the meat; wash and pat dry. Cut into 2.5 cm (1 inch) pieces and put in a bowl. Add the yogurt to the meat and mix well. Chop half the ginger with the garlic; slice the remaining ginger finely and reserve for later use. Add the chopped ginger and garlic to the meat. Add all the whole and ground spices including the salt. Stir well to coat the meat thoroughly and mix all the spices. Cover and leave to marinate at room temperature for about 4 hours.

While the meat is marinating, thaw the frozen spinach if used, or thoroughly wash and chop fresh spinach. Put the marinated meat in a heavy-based saucepan. Cook over low heat for about 45 minutes, stirring occasionally, until all the moisture has evaporated and the meat is tender. Add the spinach, mix well and cook over low heat for 2–3 minutes until the liquid has evaporated. Add 30 ml (2 level tbsp) ghee and, stirring continuously, fry the meat and spinach until the ghee starts to separate a little.

In the small frying pan, heat the remaining ghee, add the finely sliced onion and reserved sliced ginger. Stirring constantly, fry to a rich golden colour. Transfer the meat and spinach to a heated serving dish, then pour the fried onion and ginger on top and serve at once.

ROGAN JOSH

Spiced lamb in yogurt

The important flavouring in Rogan josh is mustard oil, to which ground spices and yogurt are added.

PREPARATION TIME: 35 MINUTES   COOKING TIME: 1½ HOURS   SERVES: 4–6

1 kg/2¼ lb boned tender lamb
30 ml/2 level tbsp aniseed (saunf)
1 black cardamom
45 ml/3 tbsp mustard oil
600 ml/1 pint natural yogurt (dahi)
5 ml/1 level tsp chilli powder
7.5 ml/1½ level tsp salt

1.25 ml/¼ level tsp asafoetida (hing)
4 cloves
7.5 ml/1½ level tsp dried ginger powder
2.5 ml/½ level tsp cinnamon powder
seeds from 4 green cardamoms, coarsely crushed
sprig of fresh coriander to garnish

Remove any excess fat from the lamb; wash and pat dry. Cut into 4 cm (1½ inch) pieces. Grind the aniseed and black cardamom separately to fine powder in a food processor or blender.

Heat the mustard oil to smoking point in a large heavy-based saucepan; let it smoke for a minute (to remove the pungent taste and smell) before adding the dried meat. Stirring frequently, fry the meat over medium heat to a pale golden colour. Reduce the heat slightly, add the yogurt and increase heat to medium high. Stirring constantly, fry the mixture until the oil begins to separate and float to the top. Add the chilli powder, salt, ground aniseed, asafoetida, cloves and the ground ginger. Mix all the ingredients well. Cover with a tight fitting lid, reduce the heat and simmer gently for 1¼–1½ hours until the meat is tender and the sauce has thickened. Add the ground cinnamon and the ground black cardamom. Stir well to mix the ingredients. Stirring frequently, cook for another few minutes, uncovered, so that the spices have a chance to infuse. Just before serving, sprinkle with crushed green cardamom seeds, garnish with coriander and serve really hot.

HALEEM

Wholewheat and lamb

A classic dish from Hyderabad in India, which has become a favourite in Pakistan. Wholewheat grains are first boiled and then cooked with the meat. The dish is spiced with black cumin seeds and mint. A truly unique and delicious recipe, which dates from Akbar's time in the 16th century.

PREPARATION TIME: 1 HOUR PLUS OVERNIGHT SOAKING   COOKING TIME: 2¼ HOURS
SERVES: 4–6

350 g/¾ lb wholewheat grain, washed and soaked overnight
1.6 litres/2¾ pints water
75 ml/5 level tbsp ghee
2 medium onions, skinned and finely chopped
2 garlic cloves, skinned and finely chopped
5 cm/2 inch piece fresh ginger, peeled and finely chopped
5 ml/1 level tsp black cumin seeds
4 green cardamoms

5 cloves
7.5 ml/1½ level tsp chilli powder
2.5 ml/½ level tsp ground turmeric
30 ml/2 level tbsp chopped fresh coriander leaves
15 ml/1 level tbsp chopped fresh mint leaves
450 g/1 lb boned tender lamb, cut into 2.5 cm/1 inch pieces
7.5 ml/1½ level tsp salt
300 ml/½ pint natural yogurt (dahi)
75 ml/5 tbsp lemon juice

Drain the wheat and place in a saucepan. Add 1.3 litres (2¼ pints) water and boil gently for about 45 minutes until tender and mushy. Reserve the wheat.

Heat the ghee in a large heavy-based saucepan. Add the onions and, stirring frequently, fry for about 10 minutes to a deep golden colour. Lift out all the onions with a slotted spoon. Put three quarters of them in a blender or food processor. Add the garlic and the ginger and blend to a smooth paste.

Reheat the ghee in the pan, add the ground onion mixture and continue frying for another few minutes. Then add the cumin seeds, cardamom, cloves, chilli powder, turmeric and the chopped coriander and mint. Stirring frequently, fry for 5 to 10 minutes to a rich golden colour; the ghee should start to separate.

Add the meat and the salt. Stirring frequently, fry until the meat is well browned and nearly tender, about 40 minutes. Add the yogurt and, stirring continuously, fry the meat for another 15 minutes until it is tender and the yogurt is well blended. Add the remaining 300 ml (½ pint) water, stir well and simmer for another 10 minutes. Remove the pieces of meat and chop into small pieces. Put the meat back in the sauce.

Add the boiled wheat and the strained lemon juice. Stir well to mix the ingredients. Reheat but do not allow to boil; serve at once, garnished with the reserved onion mixture.

ARBI KA SHORBA

Dasheen with lamb

Dasheen, also known as taro or arbi, is a root vegetable which is first boiled on its own, then peeled and added to the meat. Dasheen cooks quite quickly, so beware of overcooking or it will turn mushy and disintegrate.

PREPARATION TIME: 35 MINUTES   COOKING TIME: 1¼ HOURS   SERVES: 4–6

450 g/1 lb boned tender lamb
2 medium onions, skinned and chopped
2.5 cm/1 inch piece fresh ginger, peeled and chopped
2 garlic cloves, skinned
50 g/2 oz tamarind (imli), soaked in 150 ml/¼ pint
  warm water
30 ml/2 tbsp vegetable oil

5 ml/1 level tsp chilli powder
2.5 ml/½ level tsp ground turmeric
5 ml/1 level tsp salt
60 ml/4 tbsp natural yogurt (dahi)
450 ml/¾ pint water
450 g/1 lb small-sized dasheen (arbi)
15 ml/1 level tbsp finely chopped fresh coriander leaves

Cut the meat into 4 cm (1½ inch) pieces. Put the onion, ginger and garlic in a blender or food processor and blend to a smooth paste. Loosen the tamarind pulp from the fibre and strain it. Reserve the juice and discard the fibre and any pips.

Heat the oil in a heavy-based saucepan. Add the onion paste and, stirring frequently, fry for 10–15 minutes to a rich golden colour. You may add 15–30 ml (1–2 tbsp) water to prevent the mixture from sticking to the bottom of the pan. Add the chilli powder and turmeric. Stir-fry for another few minutes, then add the meat and, stirring frequently, fry the meat until well browned and nearly tender or bhoona (page 5). Season with salt.

Add a little of the yogurt and tamarind juice at a time and, stirring constantly, blend into the meat.

Repeat with remaining yogurt and juice, adding more only as the liquid is absorbed. Continue doing this until the oil starts to separate. Repeat with remaining yogurt and tamarind water. Add the water and bring to the boil. Reduce the heat, cover with a tight-fitting lid and simmer gently for about an hour or until tender.

Meanwhile, boil the dasheen until just tender. Drain and allow to cool slightly; peel and cut into halves, if too large. When the meat is tender, add the boiled dasheen. Stir gently so as not to break the pieces. Simmer gently, uncovered, for another few minutes until the dasheen absorbs some of the flavour and the sauce has reduced and thickened. Garnish with coriander.

KASHMIRI RAAN

Leg of lamb, Kashmiri-style

Pot roasting is a popular method of cooking large cuts of meat such as a whole leg of lamb. The meat, after being trimmed, is pricked right through to the bone. The success of this dish depends on the amount to which the meat has been loosened in this way: it should literally fall off the bone.

PREPARATION TIME: 1 HOUR   COOKING TIME: 2¼ HOURS   SERVES: 4–6

1 kg/2¼ lb leg of lamb
15 ml/1 level tbsp poppy seeds (khus khus)
30 ml/2 level tbsp grated fresh or desiccated coconut
2 medium onions, skinned and coarsely chopped
5 cm/2 inch piece fresh ginger, peeled and coarsely
  chopped
25 g/1 oz blanched almonds, chopped
5 cm/2 inch stick cinnamon
6 green cardamoms
3 black cardamoms, ground
4 cloves

small piece mace (javetri)
2.5 ml/½ level tsp ground nutmeg (jaiphal)
pinch asafoetida (hing)
7.5 ml/1½ level tsp chilli powder
7.5 ml/1½ level tsp salt
150 ml/¼ pint natural yogurt (dahi)
150 ml/¼ pint ghee, melted
2.5 cm/1 inch stick cinnamon
4 bay leaves, crushed
30 ml/2 level tbsp aniseed (saunf)

Remove all traces of fat and the white membrane from the meat. Prick the meat thoroughly with a sharp knife or large fork so that the fibres are completely broken up. It should virtually be falling off the bone. Place in a deep baking dish or a roasting tin.

Soak the poppy seeds and the grated coconut in a little warm water. Place the drained poppy seeds and coconut and the next 12 ingredients in a food processor or blender and blend to a smooth paste. Pour the paste over the meat and coat well all over.

Again, prick the meat very well all over to help the ground mixture to penetrate.

In another bowl, mix together the yogurt and remaining ingredients. Spread this paste over the leg of lamb. Put the lamb in the baking dish or roasting tin in a 170°C (325°F) mark 3 oven and, basting frequently, roast for about 2¼ hours. Make sure that you turn the leg over once, halfway during cooking time. Remove from the oven, transfer to a heated dish. Carve and serve hot.

KALIA

Lamb with potatoes and cauliflower

A delightful combination of meat and vegetables. The potatoes and cauliflower are first fried and then added to the meat. This is a favourite dish of the Kashmiri Muslims. Beef can be used instead of lamb.

PREPARATION TIME: 40 MINUTES PLUS 30 MINUTES' MARINATING
COOKING TIME: 1¼ HOURS   SERVES: 4

450 g/1 lb tender lamb (on the bone)
5 cm/2 inch piece fresh ginger, peeled and coarsely chopped
2 garlic cloves, skinned
2 medium onions, skinned; chop 1 finely and slice the other
450 ml/¾ pint natural yogurt (dahi)
5 ml/1 level tsp chilli powder
2.5 ml/½ level tsp ground turmeric

15 ml/1 level tbsp ground coriander
60 ml/4 level tbsp ghee
450 g/1 lb potatoes, peeled and quartered
1 small cauliflower, cut into small florets
600 ml/1 pint water
6.25 ml/1¼ level tsp salt
5 ml/1 level tsp garam masala (page 70)
30 ml/2 level tbsp finely chopped fresh coriander leaves

Trim any excess fat from the meat and cut into 4 cm (1½ inch) pieces. Wash the meat and dry it thoroughly. Place the ginger and garlic in a blender or food processor and blend to a fine paste.

Put the meat in a bowl, add the ground ginger paste, chopped onion, yogurt, chilli powder, turmeric and ground coriander. Mix all the ingredients thoroughly and leave to marinate for half an hour.

Heat the 45 ml (3 tbsp) ghee in a heavy-based pan. Add the potatoes and fry for 15 to 20 minutes to a crisp golden colour, stirring occasionally. Drain and keep aside. Add remaining ghee and fry the cauliflower florets for 10–15 minutes until

golden brown. Drain and keep aside. Add the sliced onion to the same fat and, stirring frequently, fry to a golden colour. Add the meat and the marinade. Stirring frequently, fry for 5 minutes, then add the water and salt. Mix once again and cover with a tight fitting lid. Reduce the heat and cook gently for 1¼ hours until the sauce has thickened and the meat is tender.

Add the fried potatoes and the cauliflower. Stir carefully into the meat mixture and cook for a few minutes so that they absorb some of the sauce and the flavour. Sprinkle with garam masala and coriander and serve.

KOFTE KA KORMA

Meatballs in a rich sauce

Meatballs can be made in a variety of ways, in some the mince has to be boiled first to a dry consistency. In this recipe all the lengthy boiling is eliminated. The ingredients are kneaded together to form small balls.

PREPARATION TIME: 30 MINUTES   COOKING TIME: 1 HOUR   SERVES: 4

1 garlic clove, skinned and roughly chopped
15 mint leaves, roughly chopped or 2.5 ml/½ tsp dried mint
2.5 cm/1 inch piece fresh ginger, peeled and roughly chopped
1 green chilli, roughly chopped
50 g/2 oz dried plums (aloo bukhare)
450 g/1 lb lamb or beef mince
30 ml/2 level tbsp poppy seeds (khus khus)
5 ml/1 level tsp ground aniseed (saunf)
5 ml/1 level tsp ground cumin
2.5 ml/½ level tsp chilli powder
5 ml/1 level tsp salt
oil for deep frying

Masala
3 medium onions, skinned and roughly chopped

1 garlic clove, skinned and roughly chopped
2.5 cm/1 inch piece fresh ginger, peeled and roughly chopped
1 green chilli, roughly chopped
60 ml/4 tsp oil
4 green cardamoms
6 cloves
8 whole black peppercorns
2.5 cm/1 inch stick cinnamon
1 bay leaf
10 ml/2 level tsp ground coriander
2.5 ml/½ level tsp ground turmeric
2.5 ml/½ level tsp salt
150 ml/¼ pint natural yogurt (dahi)
900 ml/1½ pints water
15 ml/1 level tbsp finely chopped fresh coriander leaves

In the blender or food processor, grind the garlic, mint, ginger and chilli to a smooth paste. Cut the plums into small pieces. Put the mince in a bowl and add the ginger paste, poppy seeds, ground aniseed, cumin, chilli powder and salt. Knead really well so that the mixture becomes firm and holds its shape.

Break off 5 ml (1 tsp) of mince mixture at a time and shape each into a smooth ball. You should be able to make 20 small meatballs. Make an indent in the centre of each one and put a piece of plum in it. Reshape into a smooth ball. Repeat in this way until all the mixture has been used up.

Heat the oil in a deep fat fryer or karhai. Add a few mince balls at a time. Turning them over, fry to an even brown colour. Drain and place on absorbent kitchen paper. Repeat with the remaining balls.

Now prepare the sauce or masala. Put the chopped onion, garlic, ginger and green chilli in a

blender or food processor and grind to a smooth paste. Heat the oil, add the paste and, stirring frequently, fry for 10–15 minutes to a rich golden brown. Add the cardamoms, cloves, black peppercorns, cinnamon and the bay leaf. Stir-fry for another few minutes until the oil separates. Then add the ground coriander, turmeric and the salt. Mix well and continue frying for another few minutes. Add the yogurt marinade, a little at a time. Stirring continuously, fry the mixture so that each batch of yogurt is thoroughly blended and the oil begins to separate.

Add the water and mix well. Bring to the boil, then reduce the heat. Simmer for 10 minutes until the sauce begins to thicken. Lower meatballs carefully in the sauce. Cover and simmer gently for about 20 minutes so that they have absorbed some of the sauce. Transfer to a heated dish, sprinkle with finely chopped coriander and serve hot.

Poultry

Chickens are one of the most popular and the cheapest sources of protein in Pakistani cookery and have none of the problems arising from religious taboos which are connected with meat. Wherever possible, use free range chickens, as their taste is far superior.

The best way to improve the flavour of poultry is by using marinades and spices, as for example, in the preparation of 'tandoori' chicken. Although its unique flavour traditionally comes from roasting the bird in a tandoor, or unglazed clay oven, a spicy yogurt- or lemon-juice-based spicy marinade does help to improve the flavour of a conventionally cooked bird.

Chicken can be cooked in a variety of ways using any number of combinations of herbs and spices. It can be cooked in a sauce or absolutely dry. It can be mild and buttery, gently piquant or fiercely hot.

TANDOORI MURGHI

Tandoori chicken

Tandoori chicken takes its name from a special unglazed clay oven or *tandoor*, which is heated with charcoal. The chicken pieces are first marinated for hours in aromatic spices and yogurt, then threaded onto skewers and roasted in the tandoor. It is the aroma of the clay and charcoal, as well as the spices, that makes this chicken a dish of distinction. A conventional oven can be used although the special aroma imparted by the clay will be missing. Chicken prepared this way is excellent cooked on an outdoor barbecue on a warm summer evening. A chicken brick is another successful alternative. Commercially produced tandoori mixes are now available in most supermarkets and make a good substitute for the homemade version.

PREPARATION TIME: 20 MINUTES PLUS 5–6 HOURS' MARINATING
COOKING TIME: 1¼ HOURS   SERVES: 4

4 chicken quarters, skinned
30 ml/2 tbsp lemon juice
1 garlic clove, skinned
2.5 cm/1 inch piece fresh ginger, peeled and coarsely
    chopped
1 green chilli
15 ml/1 tbsp water
60 ml/4 tbsp natural yogurt (dahi)

5 ml/1 level tsp ground cumin
5 ml/1 level tsp garam masala (page 70)
15 ml/1 level tsp paprika
5 ml/1 level tsp salt
a few drops of yellow food colouring
30 ml/2 level tbsp ghee, melted
lemon wedges and onion rings for garnish

Using a sharp knife, make 3 or 4 deep incisions in each chicken quarter. Put the chicken in an oven-proof dish, add the lemon juice and rub it into the incisions. Cover and marinate for half an hour. Put garlic, ginger and green chilli and water in a blender or food processor and grind to a smooth paste. Add the paste to the yogurt, ground cumin, garam masala, paprika, salt, food colouring and the melted ghee. Mix all the ingredients, then pour them over the marinated chicken pieces. Coat the pieces liberally with the yogurt marinade. Cover and leave to marinate at room temperature for 5 hours. Turn once or twice. Place the chicken in a 170°C (325°F) mark 3 oven. Roast for 1 hour, basting frequently and turning once. At the end of cooking time, the chicken should be tender and most of the marinade will have evaporated. Alternatively, grill the chicken over hot charcoal, or roast it in a chicken brick (follow manufacturer's instructions). Garnish with lemon wedges and onion rings.

VARIATION
Cut 4 chicken breasts into 5 cm (2 inch) pieces then marinate as in the tandoori recipe. Thread closely on metal skewers then proceed as above.

MURGH KORMA

Hyderabadi chicken korma

Kormas have become popular all over the world, in fact, wherever there is a restaurant from the subcontinent. But each region of Pakistan presents a different Korma – there is a story of a grand chef who claimed to be able to cook a different version for every day of the month. Hyderabadi Korma is different from any other in its use of spices such as poppy seeds.

PREPARATION TIME: 25 MINUTES   COOKING TIME: 1¼ HOURS   SERVES: 4

50 g/2 oz chirongi nuts or blanched almonds
50 g/2 oz poppy seeds (khus khus)
50 g/2 oz fresh coconut, grated
4 medium onions, skinned and coarsely chopped
2.5 cm/1 inch piece fresh ginger, peeled and coarsely chopped
2 garlic cloves, skinned
45 ml/3 level tbsp ghee
1–1.1 kg/2¼ lb chicken, skinned and cut into 8 pieces
60 ml/4 level tbsp coarsely chopped coriander leaves

15 ml/1 level tbsp fresh chopped mint leaves, washed or 2 level tsp/10 ml dried mint
30 ml/2 tbsp ground coriander
2.5 ml/½ level tsp ground turmeric
5 ml/1 level tsp chilli powder
5 ml/1 level tsp garam masala (page 70)
5 ml/1 level tsp salt
45 ml/3 tbsp lemon juice
120 ml/8 tbsp natural yogurt (dahi)
450 ml/¾ pint water

Dry-roast the chirongi nuts or almonds and the poppy seeds in a frying pan or under a grill until the nuts are a pale golden. Put them in a blender or food processor with the grated coconut; blend to a paste. Keep aside.

Blend the onions, ginger and the garlic. Heat the ghee in a large, heavy-based saucepan, add the onion paste and, stirring frequently, fry until golden. Add the chicken and, stirring frequently, fry to a gold colour or until all the moisture has evaporated.

Meanwhile, blend the coriander leaves and mint to a smooth paste. Add all the spices, the salt and the lemon juice and blend together. Add this mixture to the chicken and, stirring frequently, fry for about 10 minutes so that the chicken is well coated with the spices. Add the coconut mixture and stir in well. Stirring continuously, add a little yogurt at a time to the chicken to blend it into the mixture. Repeat until all the yogurt has been added (this will prevent it from curdling and also help to thicken the sauce). Continue stirring for 3–5 minutes and fry until the ghee begins to separate.

Pour in just enough water to cover the chicken, cover the pan, reduce the heat and allow to cook for another 20–30 minutes or until the chicken is really tender. Transfer to a heated serving dish and serve hot.

MURGH KABOLI POSANI

Chicken kaboli Posani

A few years ago I had the good fortune of staying with Maharaj Karan and his family in the old palace in the heart of Hyderabad in India. Posani, the family cook, prepared one mouth-watering dish after another during my short stay and this is one of her recipes. It can also be made with lamb or beef.

PREPARATION TIME: 35 MINUTES   COOKING TIME: 45 MINUTES   SERVES: 4

4 chicken breasts, skinned
10 ml/2 level tsp poppy seeds (khus khus)
2 garlic cloves, skinned and roughly chopped
2.5 cm/1 inch piece fresh ginger, peeled and roughly chopped
1 green chilli
225 g/8 oz fresh tomatoes, skinned and seeded
150 ml/¼ pint natural yogurt (dahi)
30 ml/2 tbsp vegetable oil
2 small slivers mace (javetri)

large pinch freshly grated nutmeg (jaiphal)
2.5 ml/½ level tsp ground cardamom
2.5 ml/½ level tsp ground cinnamon
5 ml/1 level tsp ground cumin
5 ml/1 level tsp ground coriander
6.25 ml/1¼ level tsp salt
2.5 ml/½ level tsp freshly ground black pepper
5 ml/1 level tsp ground almonds
150 ml/¼ pint double cream
30 ml/2 level tbsp finely chopped fresh coriander leaves

Cut the chicken breasts into 5 cm (2 inch) pieces. Keep aside. Soak the poppy seeds in a little warm water. Place the chopped garlic, fresh ginger, green chilli, tomatoes, yogurt and the strained poppy seeds in a blender or food processor and grind to a smooth purée.

Heat the oil in a heavy-based saucepan, pour in the tomato purée and, stirring frequently, fry this mixture over a medium heat for 5–10 minutes until the sauce begins to thicken and the oil begins to separate.

Add the chicken pieces and, stirring constantly, coat them liberally with the tomato mixture and cook them for about 15 minutes until the pieces are tender. Then add the mace, nutmeg, cardamom, cinnamon, cumin, coriander, salt and black pepper. Stirring constantly, mix the spices together and cook for another 10 minutes. Add the ground almonds. Mix them into the sauce, before pouring in the double cream.

Reduce the heat to low and continue stirring to mix in the cream. Care must be taken not to boil the cream, but just heat it through. Sprinkle the finely chopped coriander leaves on top and serve.

SHAHI MURGH BADAAMI

Royal chicken in almond sauce

A dish fit for an emperor, hence the name. The slivered almonds and the onions are sautéed to a pale golden colour so that the sauce retains its creamy appearance. A subtly flavoured dish.

PREPARATION TIME: 35 MINUTES   COOKING TIME: 1¼ HOURS   SERVES: 4

75 ml/5 tbsp vegetable oil
1–1.1 kg/2¼ lb chicken, skinned and cut in 8 pieces
100 g/4 oz blanched almonds, cut into slivers
225 g/8 oz medium onions, skinned and finely sliced
30 ml/2 level tbsp coriander seeds
8 green cardamoms

10 ml/2 level tsp poppy seeds (khus khus)
2.5 ml/½ level tsp chilli powder
5 ml/1 level tsp salt
150 ml/¼ pint water
300 ml/½ pint natural yogurt (dahi)

Heat 45 ml (3 tbsp) of the oil in a large shallow heavy saucepan. Add 4 chicken pieces and, turning frequently, fry over medium heat until golden. Drain and keep aside. Repeat with the remaining chicken pieces.

Add the remaining oil, bring it to just hot, add 15 ml (1 level tbsp) slivered almonds and fry to a pale golden colour. Drain and keep aside. Then add the sliced onions and reduce the heat to low. Stirring constantly, fry the onions to a very pale golden colour, taking care not to let them get brown as this will alter the creamy colour of the sauce. Add the remaining slivered almonds, coriander seeds, cardamoms, and the poppy seeds. Stirring constantly, fry for another 5 minutes until the almonds are a pale golden colour (do not overbrown). Add the chilli powder and salt, stir it well and remove from the heat.

Allow the mixture to cool slightly, then transfer to a blender or food processor and add the water. Blend to a smooth purée (the almonds will remain a little grainy). Return the almond mixture to the pan, add the chicken pieces. Stir well to coat the chicken pieces and to heat the sauce through. Add 30 ml (2 tbsp) of yogurt at a time and stir well into the chicken mixture. Repeat until all the yogurt has been used and is well blended.

Cover the pan with a tight fitting lid and reduce the heat. Simmer gently for about 50 minutes until the chicken is really tender, the sauce has thickened and the oil has begun to separate. It is the separation of the oil that gives the dish its glaze. Transfer to a heated dish, sprinkle with the lightly fried almonds and serve.

MURGHI MAKHAN WALI

Buttered chicken

The classic combination of onions and garlic has not been used to make the sauce in this recipe. Instead it is made with unsalted butter and thick cream, to which ground spices such as cumin and garam masala have been added. This dish is served warm, for if heated to a high temperature the cream will separate and curdle.

PREPARATION TIME: 10–15 MINUTES   COOKING TIME: 40 MINUTES   SERVES: 4

2.5 cm/1 inch fresh ginger, peeled and coarsely chopped
225 g/8 oz ripe tomatoes, skinned
1 green chilli, coarsely chopped
10 ml/2 tsp tomato purée
150 ml/¼ pint double cream
150 ml/¼ pint single cream
75 g/3 oz unsalted butter
1–1.1 kg/2¼ lb chicken, skinned and cut in 8 pieces
15 ml/1 level tbsp ground cumin
10 ml/2 level tsp paprika
5 ml/1 level tsp salt
5 ml/1 level tsp garam masala (page 70)
30 ml/2 level tbsp finely chopped fresh coriander leaves

Put the chopped ginger, tomatoes, green chilli and tomato purée in a blender or food processor and blend to a smooth paste. Mix the single and double cream together.

Melt the butter in a large heavy sauté pan. As soon as the froth subsides, add the chicken pieces, four at a time, and sauté them over medium heat for about 20–25 minutes until golden, turning once. Remove from the pan and keep warm. Repeat with the remaining chicken pieces. Reduce the heat to low, add the ground cumin and the paprika and stir-fry for a few seconds. Then add the tomato and ginger mixture and continue stirring for 3–5 minutes until the sauce thickens and is well blended.

Pour the cream into the pan and add the salt. Blend thoroughly (do not boil the sauce or cream will curdle). Add the sautéed chicken pieces and any of the juice that may have collected in the bowl. Heat the chicken and sauce gently, stirring very carefully. Add the garam masala and chopped coriander and stir carefully to mix the ingredients. Transfer to a heated dish and serve warm rather than piping hot.

TALI MURGHI

Fried chicken

An unusual dish from Bengal which has now become a favourite. Sugar is added to give a slightly sweet taste.

PREPARATION TIME: 30 MINUTES   COOKING TIME: 1 HOUR 10 MINUTES   SERVES: 4

3 medium onions, skinned and coarsely chopped
2.5 cm/1 inch piece fresh ginger, peeled and chopped
2 garlic cloves, skinned
2 green chillies
60 ml/4 level tbsp ghee
1–1.1 kg/2¼ lb chicken, skinned and cut in 8 pieces
150 ml/¼ pint water
5 ml/1 level tsp salt
15 ml/1 level tbsp sugar

Place the onion, ginger, garlic and green chillies in a blender or food processor and blend to a paste. Heat half of the ghee in a large, shallow, heavy-based pan. When hot, carefully place the chicken pieces in it, making sure that they fit in one layer in the pan and do not overlap.

Spoon the ground onion mixture on top, completely covering the chicken. Add the water and salt, bring to the boil. Reduce the heat and cook for about 45 minutes until the chicken is tender and the liquid has evaporated. Scrape off the sauce from the chicken and leave it in the pan. Carefully lift out the chicken pieces and place on absorbent kitchen paper.

Heat the remaining ghee almost to smoking point in a large frying pan. Add chicken pieces and fry for 20 minutes, turning once, until a rich golden colour; keep aside. Sprinkle the sugar into the hot ghee, add the onion sauce and, stirring constantly, fry for about 5 minutes, then add the fried chicken pieces. Coat them well with the small amount of sauce, and cook for another few minutes. Serve hot.

MURGH MUSSALLAM

Stuffed chicken in a creamy sauce

Many versions of this classic royal dish exist all over the sub-continent. The spices are fried or dry-roasted then ground into a paste made rich with cashew nuts, almonds and raisins. This mixture is then stuffed into the chicken, which is gently simmered in milk and finally thickened with natural yogurt. Although it takes time to prepare, this dish is well worth it.

PREPARATION TIME: 35 MINUTES PLUS 4–5 HOURS' MARINATING
COOKING TIME: 2 HOURS   SERVES: 4–6

Marinade
1 medium onion, skinned and coarsely chopped
2 garlic cloves, skinned and coarsely chopped
1 green chilli, coarsely chopped
60 ml/4 tbsp natural yogurt (dahi)
2.5 ml/½ level tsp salt
1–1.1 kg/2½ lb chicken, skinned

Stuffing
40 g/1½ oz basmati rice
1 egg, hard-boiled, shelled and quartered
25 g/1 oz fresh or frozen peas
1 small onion, skinned and finely chopped
1 cm/½ inch piece fresh ginger, peeled and finely chopped
50 g/2 oz blanched almonds, cut in slivers
10 ml/2 level tsp finely chopped fresh coriander leaves

Masala
4 medium onions, skinned and coarsely chopped
2.5 cm/1 inch piece fresh ginger, peeled and coarsely chopped
2 garlic cloves, skinned and coarsely chopped
75 ml/5 level tbsp ghee
8 cloves
10 black peppercorns
6 green cardamoms
5 cm/2 inch stick cinnamon
2 bay leaves
5 ml/1 level tsp salt
15 ml/1 level tbsp ground coriander
3.75 ml/¾ level tsp chilli powder
3.75 ml/¾ level tsp ground turmeric
25 g/1 oz poppy seeds (khus khus)
50 g /2 oz blanched almonds, finely chopped
25 g/1 oz green raisins (kishmish)
150 ml/¼ pint natural yogurt (dahi)
30 ml/2 level tbsp finely chopped fresh coriander leaves

Prepare the marinade for the chicken. In a blender or food processor blend the chopped onion, garlic and green chilli to a paste. Mix with 60 ml (4 tbsp) yogurt and salt in a bowl. Add the chicken, spoon the mixture over it and leave to marinate at room temperature for 4–5 hours.

Meanwhile, prepare the stuffing. Put the rice in a sieve and wash under a running cold tap until the water runs clear. Drain and put in a heavy saucepan. Level the rice with a spatula and add just enough water to cover the rice by about 2.5 cm (1 inch). Cover with a tight-fitting lid, reduce the heat and cook for about 15–20 minutes until the rice is tender and all the moisture has completely evaporated.

Mix the cooked rice, eggs, peas, onion, ginger, almonds and coriander leaves together. Remove the chicken from the marinade. Reserve the marinade for later use. Stuff the chicken with the rice mixture. Truss the chicken and keep aside.

Now prepare the sauce or masala. In a blender or food processor blend the chopped onions, ginger and garlic to a paste. Heat the ghee, add the ground onion mixture, and, stirring frequently, fry for

5–10 minutes to a rich golden colour. Add the next 5 ingredients and, stirring frequently to prevent the mixture from sticking to the bottom, fry to a rich golden colour. At this stage ghee should start to separate from the mixture.

Add the salt, ground coriander, chilli powder, turmeric and the poppy seeds. Stirring continuously, fry until the ghee separates again. Add the blanched almonds and green raisins. Combine the plain yogurt with the reserved yogurt marinade and, stirring continuously, add a little at a time to the onion and spice mixture (slow addition will prevent the yogurt from curdling). Once all the yogurt has been added, keep on stirring for another few minutes until the ghee separates once again. Remove from the heat and keep aside.

Put the stuffed chicken in a deep ovenproof dish. Cover chicken with the prepared masala and see that it is completely coated. Cover the dish and place in the oven at 180°C (350°F) mark 4. Basting frequently, cook until tender, about 1 hour. Remove the string and transfer the chicken to a heated serving dish, pour the sauce over it and serve at once. Sprinkle with coriander.

TALIHUI MURGHI

Spicy fried chicken

Lemon juice is used as a marinade for this delicious dish. Bite-sized pieces of chicken breast are preferable, but you can also use drumsticks or even wings.

PREPARATION TIME: 10–15 MINUTES PLUS 1 HOUR MARINATING
COOKING TIME: 30 MINUTES   SERVES: 4–6

4 chicken breasts, boned and skinned
60 ml/4 tbsp lemon juice
2 medium onions, skinned
45 ml/3 tbsp vegetable oil
5 cm/2 inch piece fresh ginger, peeled and cut into
    2.5 cm/1 inch-long strips

1 garlic clove, skinned and crushed
5 ml/1 level tsp ground cumin
10 ml/2 level tsp ground coriander
5 ml/1 level tsp garam masala (page 70)
2.5 ml/½ level tsp chilli powder
5 ml/1 level tsp salt

Cut chicken breasts into small 2.5 cm (1 inch) pieces. Place in a bowl with the lemon juice, mix well, cover and leave to marinate for 1 hour at room temperature. Quarter the onions and separate the layers.

Heat the oil in a deep frying pan or karhai, add the onions, the ginger and garlic and stirring frequently, fry over medium heat for 3–5 minutes until the onions become a pale golden colour.

Remove the chicken pieces from the marinade,

discard the lemon juice and add the pieces to the pan. Stirring frequently, fry the chicken for 10–15 minutes until the pieces turn a rich golden colour. Carefully drain off most of the oil leaving about 15 ml (1 tablespoon) in the pan.

Reduce the heat and add the ground cumin, ground coriander, garam masala, chilli powder and the salt. Keep tossing and fry the mixture for another 10 minutes. Transfer at once to a heated serving dish and serve hot.

SUFAID MURGH

Chicken cooked in coconut cream

Thick coconut milk and sesame seeds add a delicious flavour to the chicken, and a delicate cream colour to the dish.

PREPARATION TIME: 20–25 MINUTES   COOKING TIME: 25 MINUTES   SERVES: 4

45 ml/3 tbsp sesame oil (til ka tail)
4 chicken breasts, skinned and boned and cut in
    5 cm/2 inch pieces
2 medium onions, skinned and finely sliced
1 garlic clove, skinned and finely sliced
2.5 cm/1 inch piece fresh ginger, peeled and cut into
    thin strips
2 green chillies, finely chopped

15 ml/1 level tbsp sesame seeds (til)
6 cloves
2.5 cm/1 inch stick of cinnamon
5 ml/1 level tsp salt
300 ml/½ pint thick coconut milk (page 69)
150 ml/¼ pint thin coconut milk (page 69)
15 ml/1 level tbsp finely chopped fresh coriander leaves

Heat the sesame oil in a heavy-based deep sauté pan. Add the chicken pieces, a few at a time, and turning frequently, fry for 10 to 15 minutes until golden brown. Remove with a slotted spoon and keep warm. Repeat with remaining pieces. Add the sliced onion, garlic, ginger, green chillies, sesame seeds, cloves and cinnamon. Reduce the heat and, stirring constantly, for about 5 minutes, fry until the onion mixture is pale golden (the onions should not be dark brown or they will spoil the

colour of the sauce).

Add the salt and the thick and thin coconut milk and stir well. Bring just to boiling point and add the chicken pieces; spoon the sauce over the chicken. Reduce the heat and cook uncovered for about 10 minutes, stirring occasionally, until the chicken is really tender and the sauce has thickened. Transfer to a heated dish, sprinkle with finely chopped coriander and serve hot.

Tandoori murghi

KHADE MASALE KI MURGHI

Chicken cooked with whole spices

This dish uses whole rather than ground aromatic spices. The flavour of the chicken is enhanced by chopped almonds and fresh coriander which are added during cooking instead of as a garnish.

PREPARATION TIME: 35 MINUTES   COOKING TIME: 1¼ HOURS   SERVES: 4

50 ml/4 level tbsp ghee
450 g/1 lb onions, skinned and finely chopped
10 ml/2 level tsp cumin seeds
8 whole black peppercorns
8 cloves
5 cm/2 inch stick cinnamon
3 bay leaves
2 whole black cardamoms
50 g/2 oz blanched almonds, chopped

10 ml/2 level tbsp finely chopped fresh coriander
  leaves
1–1.1 kg/2½ lb chicken, skinned and cut in 8 pieces
2.5 ml/½ level tsp ground turmeric
5 ml/1 level tsp chilli powder
5 ml/1 level tsp salt
225 g/8 oz ripe tomatoes, finely chopped
600 ml/1 pint water

Heat the ghee in a large heavy-based frying pan and add the onions. Stirring frequently, fry the onions for 5–10 minutes until a rich golden brown – if necessary, add about 15–30 ml (1–2 tbsp) water to prevent the mixture from sticking to the bottom of the pan and burning.

Add the whole spices and continue frying for another few minutes. Add the chopped almonds and coriander leaves. Stir them into the onion mixture and then add the chicken and turmeric. Stirring frequently, fry the chicken pieces for 20 minutes until they are well browned on all sides. Add the chilli powder, salt and the chopped tomatoes. Stir for another few minutes, pour in the water, increase the heat and bring it to the boil. Reduce the heat, and simmer gently for 35–40 minutes until the chicken is tender and the sauce has thickened slightly.

MURGHI HARE MASALE KI

Chicken in green herbs and spices

A deliciously flavoured dish with fresh green herbs and spring onions.

PREPARATION TIME: 20 MINUTES   COOKING TIME: 45 MINUTES–1 HOUR
(LESS IN A PRESSURE COOKER)   SERVES: 4

4 bunches spring onions (about 30)
5 ripe medium tomatoes
45 ml/3 tbsp vegetable oil
8 chicken portions, skinned
5 cm/2 inch piece fresh ginger, peeled and cut in 2.5
  cm (1 inch) long thin strips

2 garlic cloves, skinned and crushed
60 ml/4 level tbsp finely chopped fresh coriander leaves
2 green chillies, finely chopped
5 ml/1 level tsp salt
150 ml/¼ pint water

Remove any limp or discoloured onion stalks and cut off the roots. Cut the onions into 5 cm (2 inch) pieces. Skin the tomatoes, remove and discard the pulp and coarsely chop them. Heat the oil in large, heavy-based pan. Add the chicken and, stirring continuously, fry for 20–25 minutes over medium heat to a golden brown. Add rest of the ingredients except the water and stir-fry for 10 minutes until they are well mixed and the onions begin to soften slightly. Add the water. Mix well and cover with a tight fitting lid. Reduce the heat and cook for 25 minutes or until the chicken is really tender.

Lal tamatar ke chaval, Jhinge wale chaval and Sada garam masale ke chaval

Fresh vegetables and Dals

FRESH VEGETABLES

Pakistan is a fairly large country and the climate varies enormously from North to South, hence this affects the crops and varieties of vegetables available during the different seasons.

The migration of ethnic communities to the West has meant that various tropical vegetables and fruits are becoming increasingly available here in greengrocers and supermarkets. It is interesting to note that fruits and vegetables that are still considered exotic in the West (such as okra or yams) are commonplace in the East, while our daily fare – carrots, cauliflowers or peas – are deemed a luxury in the tropics since they grow only during the short winter months. Many housewives in Pakistan sun-dry winter vegetables to preserve them for use during the summer, as domestic freezers are still a thing of the future.

Cooking vegetables

Whether boiled, steamed, sautéed or cooked in a sauce, one thing that all Pakistani vegetable dishes have in common is that they are always flavoured with some spice or other. As in western cookery, vegetables are eaten as dishes in their own right, or used for stuffings or cooked with meat, poultry, fish or dal. They also crop up in desserts, as in the case of Carrot Halva (page 67).

KHATI ARBI

Dasheen spiced with mango

Like yam, arbi or dasheen (also known as taro), has a rather bland flavour but the dried mango powder added towards the end of cooking in this dish adds a piquant touch to the vegetable. It is best to boil dasheen in its skin, then peel and cut it up as required.

PREPARATION TIME: 10 MINUTES   COOKING TIME: 40 MINUTES   SERVES: 4

450 g/1 lb small dasheen (arbi)
30 ml/2 tbsp sesame oil (til ka tail)
2.5 ml/½ level tsp cumin seeds
5 ml/1 level tsp white mustard seeds
2 medium onions, skinned and coarsely sliced
2 green chillies, finely sliced

1.25 ml/¼ level tsp chilli powder
4 curry leaves
5 ml/1 level tsp salt
10 ml/2 level tsp dried mango powder
15 ml/1 level tsp finely grated coconut

Wash the dasheen thoroughly. Boil in plenty of salted water for about 20 minutes until tender. When cool enough to handle, peel and quarter lengthwise. Keep aside.

Heat the oil in a frying pan and add the cumin and mustard seeds. They should pop and splutter at once. Add the sliced onions and green chillies, chilli powder and the curry leaves, stirring fre-quently until the onions begin to change colour. Add the quartered arbi and the salt. Continue stirring from time to time and fry the mixture, uncovered, for about 10 minutes. Finally, add the dried mango powder and the grated coconut. Stirring constantly, fry the mixture for another 5 minutes so that the vegetables are coated with the mango powder and finely grated coconut.

SHULGUM KA KORMA

Turnips with almonds and yogurt

During the winter months when turnips are plentiful and sweet, they can be used either on their own or combined with meat, poultry and, indeed, fish. Yogurt is an ideal ingredient to transform the humble turnip into something grand.

PREPARATION TIME: 20 MINUTES   COOKING TIME: 25–30 MINUTES   SERVES: 4

450 g/1 lb tender turnips (shulgum)
150 g/¼ pint natural yogurt (dahi)
3–4 unblanched almonds
15 ml/1 level tbsp desiccated coconut, moistened with a
   little warm water
5 ml/1 level tsp poppy seeds
5 ml/1 level tsp sesame seeds
10 ml/2 level tsp coriander seeds

2 garlic cloves, skinned
1.25 cm/½ inch piece fresh ginger, peeled
5 ml/1 level tsp salt
3.75 ml/¾ level tsp chilli powder
45 ml/3 tbsp oil
2 medium sized onions, skinned and finely sliced
150 ml/¼ pint water

Peel the turnips and cut into quarters if small, and eighths if large. Lightly beat the yogurt to a smooth consistency. In a blender or food processor grind together the almonds, coconut, seed spices, garlic and ginger to a smooth paste (use little water if necessary). Add the ground mixture, salt and chilli powder to the yogurt and keep aside.

Heat the oil in a heavy-based saucepan. Add the onions and, stirring frequently, fry them until a pale golden colour, taking care not to over-brown them. Add the turnips and, stirring frequently, fry them to a pale golden colour. Add the yogurt mixture and, stirring continuously, bring it to simmering point, making sure that the yogurt does not separate. Pour in the water, mix well, then cover with a tight fitting lid. Reduce the heat and allow to simmer gently until the oil separates and floats to the top and the sauce has thickened.

PALAK KA BAGHARA SALAN

Spinach with green chillies

If fresh spinach is not available use either the frozen or canned variety, although the latter may not have the same colour. The flavouring is green chillies, but be careful when adding them as their strength can vary. Seed them if you prefer a less fiery taste.

PREPARATION TIME: 20 MINUTES   COOKING TIME: 35 MINUTES   SERVES: 4–6

900 g/2 lb fresh spinach leaves, washed and coarsely
   chopped
2 garlic cloves, skinned
1.25 cm/½ inch piece fresh ginger, peeled
30 ml/2 tbsp oil

2 medium sized onions, skinned and finely sliced
3–4 green chillies, finely chopped
1.25 ml/¼ level tsp turmeric
5 ml/1 level tsp salt
150 ml/¼ pint water (optional)

If the spinach leaves are very small and tender then leave them whole; if large and slightly coarse, chop them. Wash thoroughly in a few changes of water.

In a blender or food processor grind the garlic and ginger to a fine paste. Heat the oil in a heavy-based saucepan and, stirring frequently, fry the onion to a golden colour. Add the ground ginger and garlic to the onions. Stir fry for another few minutes then add the green chillies. Fry them for a minute or two then add the turmeric and the salt. Stir well and finally add the spinach. Mix well, cover with a tight fitting lid, reduce the heat and cook until the spinach is really tender and all the moisture has dried up.

It may be necessary to add extra water from time to time to prevent the spinach from sticking. It is ready to serve when the oil begins to float to the top.

DAHI AUR PHALI KA SALAN

French beans with yogurt

A delicately spiced dish that goes well with stronger flavoured dishes.

PREPARATION TIME: 15 MINUTES   COOKING TIME: 20 MINUTES   SERVES: 4

450 g/1 lb fresh or frozen green beans
1 garlic clove, skinned
1.25 cm/½ inch piece fresh ginger
1 green chilli
30 ml/2 tbsp oil

2.5 ml/½ level tsp cumin seed
2 medium onions, skinned and finely chopped
150 ml/¼ pint yogurt (dahi), lightly beaten
5 ml/1 level tsp salt

Top and tail the fresh green beans to remove any strings. If too long cut them into 5 cm (2 inch) pieces. If frozen beans are being used thaw them completely so that any excess moisture is drained away.

In a blender or food processor grind the garlic, ginger and green chilli to a fine paste. Heat the oil in a deep frying pan or a small karhai. Add the cumin seeds and as soon as they pop and splutter, add the onions and fry, stirring frequently, until a golden colour.

Add the garlic paste to the onions, stir fry for another few minutes, then add the green beans. Stir well and cook for about 5 minutes before adding the lightly beaten yogurt and salt. Mix it well, cover with a tight fitting lid, reduce the heat to low and cook until the beans are tender but still retain their shape.

ALOO DUM

Potatoes roasted with spices

A popular Bengali dish which has many different variations; it can be cooked dry or with a sauce.
Choose small even-sized potatoes as these cook easily without splitting.

PREPARATION TIME: 7–10 MINUTES   COOKING TIME: 30–35 MINUTES   SERVES: 4

450 g/1 lb small potatoes, washed and scrubbed
mustard oil for deep frying
2.5 ml/½ level tsp mustard seeds
5 ml/1 level tsp cumin seeds
pinch of asafoetida (hing)
2 small bay leaves
5 ml/1 level tsp sugar
2.5 ml/½ level tsp ground turmeric
5 ml/1 level tsp salt

2.5 ml/½ tsp ground ginger
5 ml/1 level tsp ground coriander
2.5 ml/½ level tsp ground cumin
2.5 ml/½ level tsp chilli powder
2 ripe tomatoes, roughly chopped
60 ml/4 tbsp natural yogurt (dahi)
300 ml/½ pint water
2.5 ml/½ level tsp garam masala (page 70)

Boil the potatoes in their skins until they are tender but still retain their shape; peel, then place on absorbent paper to soak up excess moisture.

Heat the mustard oil to smoking point in a frying pan to remove the pungent smell and taste. Add a few potatoes and fry for 5 minutes to a rich golden colour, drain and keep hot; repeat until all the potatoes have been fried.

Place 30 ml (2 tablespoons) of the oil in a heavy-based saucepan. Heat it up to smoking point again, then add the mustard and cumin seeds, the asafoetida and the bay leaves. As soon as the seeds pop and splutter add the sugar, turmeric, salt, ground ginger, coriander, cumin, chilli powder and chopped tomatoes. Stirring constantly, fry the mixture for a few minutes, then add a little of the yogurt and stir it in really well. Fry the mixture for a few more minutes until the oil starts to separate. Repeat with the remaining yogurt, adding it in the same way, a little at a time, to prevent it from curdling.

Add the water, stir well and bring the mixture to the boil. Reduce the heat, cover and simmer gently for about 10 minutes. Add the fried potatoes and simmer for another 10 minutes so that the potatoes absorb some of the sauce. Sprinkle with garam masala, cover and leave to infuse for 2–3 minutes before serving.

BAINGAN BHARTHA

Roasted aubergines in spices

Aubergines come in a variety of shapes, sizes and colours. Some are long and thin, others round, and they can be either very small or large. Colours range from white to green, deep pink to dark purple. It is the last variety that is best for this delicious dish, whose unique flavour is traditionally obtained by roasting the aubergines over a fierce charcoal fire. As that is not always a practical proposition, the same result can be achieved by placing the aubergines over a naked gas flame or under a very hot grill. This chars the skin completely and cooks the pulp, which is then gently sautéed with onions, tomatoes and spices.

PREPARATION TIME: 20 MINUTES   COOKING TIME: 20 MINUTES   SERVES: 4

2 large, firm round aubergines, washed
45 ml/3 tbsp vegetable oil
3 medium onions, skinned and finely chopped
2.5 cm/1 inch piece fresh ginger, peeled and finely
   chopped

1 green chilli, finely chopped
1.25 ml/¼ level tsp chilli powder
6.25 ml/1¼ level tsp salt
4 large ripe tomatoes, chopped
15 ml/1 level tbsp finely chopped fresh coriander leaves

Pat dry the aubergines with absorbent kitchen paper. If using gas, spike each aubergine with a fork and hold it over the burner to char the skin. Place under a hot grill if using an electric cooker. Turn the aubergines a few times to make sure that the skin is completely charred. Remove from heat and place in a bowl until cool enough to handle. Hold the aubergine by the stalk and carefully remove all the charred skin. Do not worry if a few small pieces stick to the soft flesh. Cut off the stalk and discard. Chop remaining flesh into large pieces.

   Heat the oil in a heavy-based pan, add the onions, ginger and green chilli. Stirring frequently,

fry for 5–10 minutes to a deep golden colour without over-browning. Add the chilli powder, salt and the chopped tomatoes. Stirring frequently, fry this mixture for 5 minutes until the oil separates, then add the chopped aubergine. Mix in well and, stirring frequently, fry the mixture, uncovered, for 10–15 minutes until all the ingredients are well blended and the aubergines have absorbed the other flavours. (It is important that the pan is not covered while cooking, or the onions and aubergines will give off liquid.) Transfer to a heated serving dish, sprinkle with chopped coriander and serve.

BHINDI PIYAZ

Okra and onions

Choose okra by gently pressing a pod – it should feel firm but not hard and woody, and there should be no tiny prickly hairs which are an indication that it is overripe and has developed tough fibres which are difficult to soften in cooking. Okra cooks quickly, so don't overcook it or it will become slimy and mushy.

PREPARATION TIME: 15 MINUTES   COOKING TIME: 15–20 MINUTES   SERVES: 4

30 ml/2 tbsp vegetable oil
2.5 ml/½ level tsp cumin seeds
2 medium onions, skinned and sliced
2.5 ml/½ level tsp chilli powder
1.25 ml/¼ level tsp ground turmeric

5 ml/1 level tsp salt
450 g/1 lb tender okra, washed and cut into 1.25 cm (½
   inch) slices
2 medium ripe tomatoes, roughly chopped

In a large, heavy-based sauté pan, heat the oil over high heat; add the cumin seeds as soon as they pop and splutter add the sliced onions. Stirring frequently, fry the onions for 5–10 minutes to a deep, golden brown. Do not overbrown.

   Add the chilli powder, turmeric and the salt.

Continue frying for about 2 minutes, then add the sliced okra and chopped tomatoes. Mix well, reduce heat to low, cover and allow the vegetables to cook in their own juices, stirring once or twice for about 10 minutes until the okra is tender and keeps its shape. Serve hot.

KHATTA KADOO

Piquant yellow pumpkin

The humble pumpkin has more uses than just as a decoration at Hallowe'en. In this delicious dish, it is sautéed lightly with onions, tomatoes and spices.

PREPARATION TIME: 20 MINUTES   COOKING TIME: 45 MINUTES–1 HOUR   SERVES: 4

30 ml/2 tbsp vegetable oil
5 ml/1 level tsp cumin seeds
1.25 ml/¼ level tsp nigella seeds (kalonji)
2 medium onions, skinned and finely sliced
small piece fresh ginger, peeled and finely sliced
2.5 ml/½ level tsp chilli powder
2.5 ml/½ tsp ground turmeric

5 ml/1 level tsp salt
2 ripe tomatoes, coarsely chopped
450 g/1 lb yellow pumpkin, peeled, seeded and cut into
    pieces about 2.5 cm (1 inch) long and 1.25 cm
    (½ inch) thick
10 ml/2 level tsp dried mango powder
2.5 ml/½ level tsp garam masala (page 70)

Heat the oil in a medium-sized saucepan over high heat. Add the cumin and nigella seeds – they should pop and splutter at once. Add the sliced onion and ginger, reduce the heat and, stirring frequently, fry the onion mixture to a pale golden colour. Add the chilli powder, turmeric and salt. Stir them into the onions and fry for another minute. Then add the roughly chopped tomatoes, stir and fry for another few minutes until the tomatoes become soft.

Add the pumpkin to the onion and tomato mixture. Mix all the ingredients, cover, reduce the heat and allow to cook in its own juices until the pumpkin is soft and tender. Mash a few pieces with a fork and keep some pieces whole. Add the mango powder and the garam masala, mix well; cook for another few minutes and serve.

NADROO KI YAKHNI

Lotus stems in yogurt sauce

Lotus stems are available in cans at most grocery stores. One can occasionally buy them fresh. The outer stems look like bamboo, but when sliced have a lacy cross-section. Fresh lotus stems are first peeled, then soaked in acidulated water as they tend to discolour very quickly. In this recipe, they are boiled. In others, they can be boiled, mashed and made into kofte or balls and cooked in a piquant sauce.

PREPARATION TIME: 20 MINUTES   COOKING TIME: 45 MINUTES   SERVES: 4–6

540 g/19 oz can or 450 g/1 lb fresh lotus stems, peeled
    and cut into 1.25 cm/½ inch thick slices
600 ml/1 pint water
5 ml/1 level tsp ground ginger
15 ml/1 level tbsp ground aniseed (sauf)
2 whole large black cardamoms

2.5 ml/½ level tsp chilli powder
5 ml/1 level tsp salt
30 ml/2 tbsp mustard oil
105 ml/7 tbsp natural yogurt (dahi)
15 ml/1 tbsp finely chopped fresh coriander leaves

Add lotus stems, water, spices and salt to a saucepan. Bring to the boil, then reduce heat slightly, cover and simmer for about 20 minutes until the lotus stems are tender and a fair amount of water has evaporated.

In a small frying pan heat the mustard oil to smoking point to eliminate its pungent taste and smell. Pour this oil onto the cooked stems. Allow to cool slightly, then, stirring continuously, add only 15 ml (1 tbsp) of yogurt at a time to prevent curdling. This will blend in the yogurt and thicken the sauce. Transfer to a serving dish and serve immediately, sprinkled with fresh coriander.

JIMIKANDH KA KORMA

Yam in a spicy sauce

A large tuberous vegetable, the yam used in this recipe is also known as 'elephants' foot' or suram and is a native of India. These large tubers keep well for a long time and often have pink or slightly creamy flesh. The skin of a yam is a dirty earth colour and is very tough; it needs to be peeled off thoroughly. Yams are acrid and can sometimes cause skin irritation during peeling, so always rub a little oil – cooking oil will do – on your hands before peeling.

PREPARATION TIME: 30 MINUTES   COOKING TIME: 50 MINUTES   SERVES: 4–6

450 g/1 lb yam, peeled and cut into 2 cm/¾ inch cubes
10 ml/2 level tsp salt
2 medium onions, skinned and finely chopped
2.5 cm/1 inch piece fresh ginger, peeled and chopped
1 garlic clove, skinned and finely chopped
45 ml/3 tbsp vegetable oil
5 ml/1 level tsp cumin seeds
7.5 ml/1½ level tsp ground coriander
2.5 ml/½ level tsp chilli powder

2.5 ml/½ level tsp ground turmeric
6.25 ml/1¼ level tsp salt
2 medium tomatoes, finely chopped
30 ml/2 tbsp natural yogurt (dahi)
750 ml/1¼ pint water
oil for deep frying
2.5 ml/½ level tsp garam masala (page 70)
15 ml/1 level tbsp finely chopped fresh coriander leaves

Sprinkle the cubes of yam with salt and rub it in to extract excess water. Set aside in a colander.

In a blender or food processor grind the onion, ginger and garlic to a fine paste. Heat the vegetable oil in a heavy-based saucepan and add the cumin seeds. They should pop and splutter at once. Add the ground onion mixture and, stirring frequently, fry for 10–15 minutes until it reaches a deep golden colour (add a little water at a time to prevent the mixture from sticking to the bottom of the pan).

Add the ground coriander, chilli, turmeric and salt. Continue frying for another minute, then add the chopped tomatoes and stir-fry for a few minutes until the tomatoes are reduced to a pulp. Add the yogurt, a little at a time and, stirring constantly, blend it into the mixture (this will prevent the yogurt from curdling). Continue frying over medium heat for another few minutes until the oil starts to separate.

Pour in the water, stir well, cover and slowly bring to the boil. Simmer, uncovered, for 15 minutes so that the sauce thickens slightly.

Heat the oil in the deep fat fryer or karhai. Stand well back and drop a few of the prepared yam cubes into the hot oil. Fry, turning once or twice, to a rich golden colour. Remove with a slotted spoon, place on absorbent kitchen paper. When all the cubes are done put them in the simmering sauce. Stir once, cover and leave to simmer gently for another 15 minutes so that the fried cubes absorb some of the sauce (it will also have thickened slightly).

Five minutes before serving sprinkle in the garam masala and the coriander leaves. Stir them into the rest of the ingredients so that the spices have time to infuse.

BHAGHARE BAINGAN

Spicy aubergines

A classic dish from the stronghold of Mughlai cooking in South India. The unique feature of this dish is that the onions are first roasted in their skins, then peeled, chopped and fried. The roasting gives them a distinctive flavour.

PREPARATION TIME: 20 MINUTES   COOKING TIME: 40 MINUTES   SERVES: 4

8 small round aubergines, washed
90 ml/6 tbsp vegetable oil
2 medium onions
2.5 cm/1 inch piece fresh ginger, peeled and chopped
2 garlic cloves, skinned and chopped
10 ml/2 level tsp sesame seeds (til)
10 ml/2 level tsp poppy seeds (khus khus)
15 ml/1 level tbsp raw peanuts, shelled
5 ml/1 level tsp cumin seeds

5 ml/1 tsp ground coriander
15 ml/1 level tbsp grated coconut
2.5 ml/½ level tsp fenugreek seeds (methi dane)
4 curry leaves
2.5 ml/½ tsp ground turmeric
5 ml/1 level tsp salt
5 ml/1 level tsp chilli powder
60 ml/4 level tbsp tamarind juice (imli) (page 69)

Pat dry the aubergines. Slit them lengthwise carefully into four, leaving them still held together at the stalk. Heat the oil in a deep frying pan and gently fry the aubergines, turning once, for a few minutes until tender. Remove with a slotted spoon and keep aside on absorbent kitchen paper.

Place the onions under a hot grill. Turn them regularly to completely char the skin. Remove from heat, carefully peel away all the charred skin and chop coarsely. Place the chopped onion, ginger, garlic, sesame seeds, poppy seeds, peanuts, 2.5 ml/½ tsp cumin seeds, the ground coriander and the grated coconut in a blender or food processor and grind to a smooth paste.

Strain off all but 30 ml (2 tbsp) of the oil from the frying pan. Heat the oil and the remaining cumin seeds and the fenugreek seeds. They should pop and splutter at once. Add the curry leaves and almost at once add the ground onion mixture, turmeric, salt and the chilli powder. Fry this mixture, stirring frequently, over medium heat for about 10 minutes until the colour turns to a rich golden brown and the oil begins to separate.

Add the tamarind juice, stir well and allow to cook for another few minutes. Add the fried aubergines and carefully coat them with the mixture. Cover with a tight-fitting lid, reduce the heat to low and cook for about 15 minutes. Transfer to heated serving dish and serve at once.

MATTAR PANEER

Cottage cheese and peas in a piquant sauce

Paneer – a soft cheese that can be made in a few minutes at home – is one of the most popular sources of protein. This is a classic dish in which squares of paneer are cooked with fresh or frozen peas in an onion, ginger and garlic spice mixture or masala, which is the base of many sauces. These ingredients add a delicious flavour and also act as a thickening agent for the sauce.

PREPARATION TIME: 15 MINUTES   COOKING TIME: 40 MINUTES   SERVES: 4–6

225 g/8 oz pressed paneer (page 69)
oil for deep frying
2 medium onions, skinned and cut in quarters
2.5 cm/1 inch piece of fresh ginger, peeled and sliced
1 garlic clove, skinned
1 green chilli
100 g/4 oz fresh or canned tomatoes
225 g/8 oz fresh or frozen peas
300 ml/½ pint water

30 ml/2 tbsp vegetable oil
5 ml/1 level tsp cumin seeds
2.5 ml/½ level tsp nigella seeds (kalonji)
2.5 ml/½ level tsp chilli powder
2.5 ml/½ level tsp ground turmeric
7.5 ml/1½ level tsp ground coriander
6.25 ml/1¼ level tsp salt
15 ml/1 level tbsp chopped fresh coriander leaves
2.5 ml/½ level tsp garam masala (page 70)

Cut the pressed paneer into 1.25 cm (½ inch) cubes. Heat the oil in a deep fat fryer or karhai. Add a few cubes at a time and fry them to a pale golden colour turning once. Too much frying will make them hard and chewy. Remove with a slotted spoon and drain on absorbent paper. In a food processor or liquidiser grind together the onion, ginger, garlic and green chilli to a fine paste. If fresh tomatoes are used, chop them into small pieces. If canned, mash them slightly. Shell and wash fresh peas (there is no need to thaw frozen ones).

Heat oil in a heavy-based saucepan and add the cumin and nigella seeds. They should pop and splutter at once. Add the ground onion paste, mix well and, stirring frequently, fry over medium heat to a deep golden colour – add 15 ml (1 tbsp) of water at a time to prevent the mixture from sticking to the bottom. The oil should start to separate at this point. Add the chilli powder, turmeric, ground coriander and salt. Stir well for a few minutes then add the tomatoes. Again, stir frequ-

ently until at first the sauce absorbs the oil and then begins to release it. Add the peas to the sauce.

Stirring constantly, fry them for another few minutes. Pour in the remaining water, mix well, cover partially and bring to the boil. Reduce the heat, cover completely and allow to simmer for about 15 minutes or until the peas are tender.

Carefully drop in the fried paneer cubes. Stir gently, cover and cook for another 10 minutes until the paneer absorbs some of the flavour and the sauce becomes thicker. Finally, add the chopped coriander and the garam masala. Mix them in well. Cover and simmer for another 5 minutes before serving.

NOTE
If tomatoes are not available then use 45 ml/3 tbsp of natural yogurt. Add 15 ml (1 tbsp) of yogurt at a time and, stirring constantly, blend it in thoroughly before adding the next. This will prevent the yogurt from curdling.

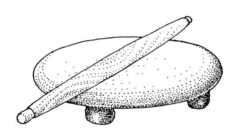

DALS

Pulses or Dals form the base of many vegetarian and non-vegetarian dishes. In Pakistani cooking, these pulses are often combined with meat or poultry to add a new dimension to their bland taste. Of course simple dals are also cooked.

The biggest selection of pulses, dried beans and peas is still available in oriental stores, though good supermarkets and healthfood stores do now stock a fairly good range. It is a known fact these ingredients can be somewhat indigestible and this is why the spices used in their cooking play a very important part. Spices such as asafoetida (hing) and ajowan seeds counteract the problem of flatulence and so a small pinch of either should always be added to whichever pulse, bean or pea is being cooked.

Pulses are classified as being whole or split, although they may belong to the same family. Red

kidney beans were the centre of controversy a few years ago when it was discovered that the tannin in them is not easily destroyed by the slow cooking process and some people became seriously ill. See *Glossary*, page 78, for cooking instructions.

Some pulses like moong and urad dal are often ground into a thick paste and then made into dumplings and deep-fried. These are added to rich spicy sauces as an alternative to fresh vegetables or immersed in plain yogurt.

Pulses are also ground into flour which can be used to make an egg-free coating batter for frying vegetables or other ingredients to a golden crispness.

They can also be ground to a thick paste and then gently roasted in ghee to make fudge and other sweetmeats. More information on pulses is provided in the *Glossary*, pages 72 to 78.

RAJMA

Red kidney beans in sauce

A popular dish in the Punjab where it is often prepared for Sunday lunch. The length of cooking time for these kidney beans has recently been the subject of much debate. They do contain a toxic substance that can only be destroyed by prolonged cooking. Therefore it is essential that they are first soaked for a good 12 hours, then boiled rapidly for 10 minutes before cooking for a further 1½ hours or for at least 20–30 minutes in the pressure cooker. They are then ready for use.

PREPARATION TIME: 20 MINUTES PLUS 12 HOURS' SOAKING
COOKING TIME: 1½ HOURS (LESS IN A PRESSURE COOKER)   SERVES: 4

225 g/8 oz red kidney beans, soaked overnight
1½ litres/3 pints water
45 ml/3 tbsp vegetable oil
5 ml/1 level tsp cumin seeds
3 medium onions, skinned and finely chopped
1 garlic clove, skinned and finely chopped
2.5 cm/1 inch piece fresh ginger, peeled and finely
    chopped

1 green chilli, finely chopped
3.75 ml/¾ level tsp chilli powder
2.5 ml/½ level tsp ground turmeric
15 ml/1 level tbsp ground coriander
100 g/4 oz fresh or half a 227 g (8 oz) can tomatoes
    with their juice, roughly chopped
7.5 ml/1½ level tsp salt
15 ml/1 tbsp finely chopped fresh coriander leaves

Drain the soaked beans and wash well. Pick them over and discard any that are still shrivelled up. Place beans in a saucepan, add water and boil rapidly for 10 minutes then boil for a further 1½ hours until tender and their skins have split. (Alternatively place in a pressure cooker, pour in half the water and cook on high pressure for at least 20 minutes or follow manufacturer's instructions.)

Prepare the spice mixture or masala. Heat the oil in a large frying pan and add the cumin seeds. They should pop and splutter at once. Add the chopped onion, garlic, ginger and chopped chilli. Stirring frequently, fry the mixture to a rich golden colour. Add the chilli powder, turmeric and ground

coriander. Stir well and continue frying for another few minutes until the oil begins to separate. Add the tomatoes and any liquid (if canned). Stir them into the mixture and fry until the oil begins to separate and the tomatoes are well mixed in.

As soon as the red kidney beans are tender add this prepared masala and give it a good stir. Cover with a lid and reduce the heat to low. Let the beans simmer gently until the masala is well blended. Mash some of the beans with a potato masher or with a wooden spoon against the side of the saucepan to thicken the sauce a little. Season to taste with salt. Transfer to a serving dish and serve hot, sprinkled with coriander leaves.

PHOOLI HUI DAL

Lemon-flavoured dal

This simple dal is flavoured with lime or lemon juice and often eaten with parathas for breakfast in many traditional Muslim homes. It has a rather dry consistency.

PREPARATION TIME: 10 MINUTES PLUS 10 MINUTES' SOAKING
COOKING TIME: 40 MINUTES   SERVES: 4

15 ml/1 tbsp sesame oil (til ka tail)
1 medium onion, skinned and finely chopped
2 cm/1 inch piece fresh ginger, peeled and finely chopped
1 small garlic clove, skinned and finely chopped
2.5 ml/½ level tsp ground turmeric
2.5 ml/½ level tsp chilli powder

3.75 ml/¾ level tsp salt
1 green chilli, finely chopped
15 ml/1 level tbsp finely chopped fresh coriander leaves
225 g/8 oz masoor dal, thoroughly washed and soaked for 10 minutes
30 ml/2 tbsp lemon juice
300 ml/½ pint water

Heat the oil in a heavy-based saucepan. Add the onion, ginger and the garlic. Stirring frequently, fry for a few minutes until the mixture turns to a pale golden colour and the onion is transparent. Add the turmeric, chilli powder, salt, green chilli and the coriander leaves. Stirring frequently, fry the mixture for 5–8 minutes to a rich golden colour. Then add the drained dal, the lemon juice and the water. Mix well, reduce the heat, cover and allow to cook for about 30 minutes or until the dal is tender and all the moisture had dried up.

MASOOR KI DAL METHI KE SATH

Masoor dal with fenugreek leaves

A delicious combination. If fresh fenugreek leaves are not available then use dried leaves, but only a quarter of the quantity of fresh ones.

PREPARATION TIME: 20 MINUTES PLUS 25 MINUTES' SOAKING
COOKING TIME: 35–40 MINUTES   SERVES: 4

450 g/1 lb fresh fenugreek leaves, washed and shaken dry
or
125 g/4 oz dried fenugreek leaves (soaked in cold water for 30 minutes)
175 g/6 oz masoor dal
1 garlic clove, skinned

1.25 cm/½ inch piece fresh ginger
1 green chilli
30 ml/2 tbsp oil
1 medium onion, skinned and finely chopped
2.5 ml/½ level tsp chilli powder
1.25 ml/¼ level tsp turmeric
5 ml/1 level tsp salt

If fresh fenugreek leaves are used then remove any coarse stalks. Chop roughly. If dried leaves are used, carefully remove the coarse dry stalks. Wash in a few changes of water. Then soak the leaves in cold water without disturbing them. When you are ready to use them, carefully scoop out just the leaves without disturbing the water at the bottom, as this is where all the grit will have settled.

Wash the dal in a few changes of water, until the water runs clear. Then leave it to soak in cold water for about 25 minutes. Drain the dal and keep aside.

In a blender or food processor grind the garlic, ginger and chilli into a paste. Heat the oil in a heavy-based saucepan and add the onion, stirring frequently fry to a golden colour.

Add the paste to the onions along with the chilli powder, turmeric and the salt and fry for another few minutes. Add the chopped fenugreek leaves and fry, stirring continuously, for a few minutes until well coated with the oil, then add the drained lentils. Mix well, then pour in enough water to cover the dal by 2.5 cm (1 inch). Cover with a tight fitting lid, reduce the heat, and leave to cook for 30 minutes or until the dal is tender and all the moisture has dried up.

KHATEE DAL AAM WALI

Moong dal with mango

During the short mango season everything and anything that can be flavoured with mangoes is cooked. If fresh unripe mangoes are not available then use the dry mango slivers or mango powder.

PREPARATION TIME: 10 MINUTES PLUS 30 MINUTES' SOAKING
COOKING TIME: 45 MINUTES (LESS IN A PRESSURE COOKER)   SERVES: 4

225 g/8 oz split moong
1–2 garlic cloves, skinned
1.25 cm/½ inch piece fresh ginger, peeled
1 medium onion, skinned and finely sliced
1–2 green unripe mangoes, peeled and grated
1 green chilli, finely chopped
5 ml/1 level tsp salt

900 ml/1½ pints water

Baghar
15 ml/1 level tbsp ghee
5 ml/1 level tsp cumin seeds
2.5 ml/½ level tsp chilli powder
30 ml/2 level tbsp freshly chopped coriander leaves

Thoroughly clean and wash the moong in a few changes of water. Leave to soak in plenty of cold water for 30 minutes. Drain and transfer it to a heavy-based saucepan.

In a blender or food processor grind the garlic and ginger together. Add the onion, grated mango, ground garlic and ginger, green chilli and the salt to the saucepan. Mix well. Add the water, cover and simmer gently until the water has been absorbed and the dal is tender and slightly mushy. Transfer to a covered serving dish.

To prepare the Baghar, heat the ghee in a small frying pan then add the cumin seeds – they should pop and splutter at once. Add the chilli powder and at once pour it over the hot dal. Replace the cover on the serving dish to let the aromas infuse. Sprinkle with the chopped coriander leaves and serve.

NOTE
If dried mango slivers are used then soak them in a little warm water for 15 minutes to soften them slightly. Add the slivers and the water to the dal.

KHAREE MOONG DAL

Moong dal with curry leaves

You may use masoor instead of moong dal for this. As very little cooking is required it is best to soak the dal for 3–4 hours to soften it.

PREPARATION TIME: 10 MINUTES PLUS 4 HOURS' SOAKING
COOKING TIME: 25–30 MINUTES   SERVES: 4

225 g/8 oz moong dal, without skins
1–2 garlic cloves, skinned
1.25 cm/½ inch piece fresh ginger, peeled
15 ml/1 tbsp ghee
1 green chilli, finely chopped
3–4 cloves

3–4 curry leaves
2.5 ml/½ level tsp chilli powder
2.5 ml/½ level tsp turmeric
5 ml/1 level tsp salt
300 ml/½ pint water
lemon wedges

Thoroughly clean and wash the dal in several changes of water. Soak in plenty of cold water for up to 4 hours. Drain and set aside.

In a blender or food processor, grind the garlic and ginger together. Heat the ghee and add the ground garlic and ginger, green chilli, cloves and the curry leaves. Stirring continuously, fry them

for a minute or so then add the drained dal, chilli powder, turmeric and salt.

Mix well, then add the water. Once again mix well, cover with a tight fitting lid, reduce the heat and simmer gently until all the water has been absorbed and the dal is tender and dry. Garnish with lemon wedges.

LOBHIA

Black-eyed beans in a piquant sauce

Although they belong to the bean family black-eyed beans do not need prolonged soaking – between 4 and 5 hours should be enough. Natural yogurt adds flavour to the basic onion, ginger and garlic base. This dish tastes better if made well in advance and then reheated just before serving.

PREPARATION TIME: 20 MINUTES PLUS 4 HOURS' SOAKING
COOKING TIME: 1¼–1½ HOURS   SERVES: 4

275 g/10 oz black-eyed beans, soaked
3 medium onions, skinned and chopped
2.5 cm/1 inch piece fresh ginger, peeled and chopped
2 garlic cloves, skinned and chopped
1 green chilli, chopped
45 ml/3 tbsp vegetable oil
5 ml/1 level tsp cumin seeds
2.5 ml/½ level tsp nigella seeds (kalonji)

2.5 ml/½ level tsp chilli powder
2.5 ml/½ level tsp ground turmeric
10 ml/2 level tsp ground coriander
5 ml/1 level tsp salt
60 ml/4 tbsp natural yogurt (dahi)
900 ml/1½ pints water
30 ml/2 level tbsp finely chopped fresh coriander leaves

Drain the soaked beans and discard any that have not swollen up to twice their size. Place the onions, ginger, garlic and the green chilli in a blender or food processor and grind to a fine paste. Heat the oil in a heavy-based saucepan, add the cumin and nigella seeds, and as soon as they pop and splutter, add the ground onion mixture and, stirring frequently, fry for 10 minutes to a rich golden brown. Add 15 ml (1 tbsp) water at a time in case the mixture starts to stick to the bottom of the pan.

Continue frying until the oil separates, then add the spices and the salt. Continue frying for another few minutes, then add a little yogurt at a time and stirring continuously, blend it in. It is important that the oil separates after each spoonful or the yogurt might curdle. By the time the last spoonful has been fried the sauce will be rich in appearance and have a glossy sheen. Add the drained black-eyed beans, stir well to mix, then add the water. Stir well, reduce the heat, cover and leave to boil gently for about 1¼–1½ hours or until the beans are tender. Add a little more water if required. Transfer to a heated serving dish and sprinkle with finely chopped coriander leaves.

KABLI CHANNE

Spicy white chick peas

A substantial dish which is cooked in an onion, ginger and garlic masala. The chick peas are soaked overnight and then boiled in plenty of water before being added to the sauce.

PREPARATION TIME: 20 MINUTES PLUS 12 HOURS' SOAKING
COOKING TIME: ABOUT 3 HOURS (LESS IN A PRESSURE COOKER)   SERVES: 4

225 g/8 oz chick peas, soaked overnight and drained
1 litre/2¾ pints water
2.5 ml/½ level tsp bicarbonate of soda
45 ml/3 tbsp vegetable oil
5 ml/1 level tsp cumin seeds
2.5 ml/½ level tsp nigella seeds (kalonji)
2.5 ml/½ level tsp mustard seeds
3 medium onions, skinned and finely chopped
2.5 cm/1 inch piece fresh ginger, peeled and finely
  chopped

2 garlic cloves, skinned and finely chopped
1 green chilli, finely chopped
5 ml/1 level tsp chilli powder
2.5 ml/½ level tsp ground turmeric
10 ml/2 level tsp ground coriander
5 ml/1 level tsp salt
100 g/4 oz fresh or canned tomatoes, roughly chopped
10 ml/2 level tsp dried mango powder
5 ml/1 level tsp garam masala (page 70)
15 ml/1 level tbsp finely chopped fresh coriander leaves

Put the chick peas in a large heavy-based saucepan, add the water and the bicarbonate of soda and bring to the boil. Stir any froth that may form back into the chick peas. Cover the pan and boil the chick peas for about 1½ hours until they are tender but still retain their shape. (This process can be speeded up in a pressure cooker. Use half the quantity of water – just enough to reach 2.5 cm (1 inch) above the chick peas. Follow the manufacturer's instructions for timing.) Once the chick peas have become tender keep them in the boiled water, as that is also used.

Heat the oil in a large frying pan. Add the cumin, nigella and mustard seeds – they should pop and splutter at once. Add the finely chopped onions, ginger, garlic and green chilli. Stirring frequently, fry the mixture for 10–15 minutes until well browned. Add the chilli powder, turmeric, ground coriander and salt. Stir-fry for another few minutes then add the tomatoes (and liquid if canned). Stir frequently and fry until the tomatoes are reduced to a pulp and well mixed, about 5 minutes; the oil should start to separate at this point.

Pour the onion mixture into the cooked chick peas and their liquid. Stir well to mix all the ingredients, sprinkle with dried mango powder and cover with a lid. Reduce heat and simmer for 45 minutes or until the chick peas have absorbed the sauce. Mash a few of the chick peas with a potato masher or with the back of a wooden spoon against the side of the pan to thicken the sauce. Transfer the chick peas to a heated serving dish, sprinkle with the garam masala and the finely chopped fresh coriander leaves and serve hot.

Rice and Bread

Rice

The contribution of the sub-continent to the repertoire of rice dishes is enormous: every region has added something unique in the way of flavouring. Rice dishes can be served as starters, main meals, supplements to the main meal, snacks to serve at teatime or with drinks and as desserts. Rice can also be ground into flour and made up into batter or pancakes.

There are several varieties of rice and the size (short, medium and long) and the thickness of the grain determines the quality and the taste of a prepared dish. Patna or other long-grained rice with slightly rounded sides, is most commonly used for everyday cooking, while the delicately aromatic, basmati rice is chiefly used in special dishes. Basmati is often considered to be the king of rice, and is sometimes left for 10–15 years to mature.

In Pakistani cookery, rice should be light and fluffy with each and every grain separate. This may sound like a counsel of perfection, but a number of factors contribute to this effect: the type of rice, the duration of soaking, number of washes, the amount of water used and so on.

On the subject of washing and soaking, there are different schools of thought. Some say that rice should never be washed, let alone soaked. Others recommend that it should be washed thoroughly until the water runs clear (to remove any excess starch and any white polishing powder) and then soaked for 20–30 minutes so that on cooking it will require less water. I find that with the exception of a few dishes, I agree with the second school of thought. I wash the rice gently but thoroughly, taking care not to break the grains, in a few changes of water or until the water runs clear. I then soak it in cold water for 20–30 minutes.

After washing and soaking, there are two very distinct methods of cooking rice.

1. Boil it in plenty of lightly salted water, and when the rice is tender, drain off the water. Rinse the rice in clear water, heat it through and serve. A good way of getting rid of the excess starch. This method is fine when dealing with glutinous rice, but would be sacrilege for basmati, whose delicate flavour would be lost.

2. The best way to cook basmati rice is to wash it well and soak in plenty of cold water. Drain the rice carefully and place it in a saucepan. Level the surface with a spatula and carefully pour in enough water to cover the rice by about 2.5 cm (1 inch). The easiest way to measure the level is by dipping a clean index finger into the water until the tip of your finger touches the rice. The water should reach the first joint of your finger. Add salt, cover the rice, reduce the heat and cook gently for 20 minutes over low heat *without opening the lid*. This method ensures perfectly cooked light and fluffy rice with each grain separate from the next.

With parboiled, boil-in-the-bag and any of the other processed rice now available in the market, it is best to follow the instructions.

SAABAT GARAM MASALE KE CHAVAL

Aromatic spice pullao

Garam masala literally means 'warm spices'. The five basic warm spices have a different and altogether milder temperament compared to the lethal fire of chillies. The five garam masala spices are cardamom (green or black), cloves, cinnamon, bay leaves and black pepper and they can either be used whole or in ground form. I have used them whole to add a subtle warmth rather than a burning sensation to this pullao.

PREPARATION TIME: 5–10 MINUTES PLUS 30 MINUTES' SOAKING
COOKING TIME: 20–25 MINUTES   SERVES: 4–6

275 g/10 oz basmati rice
15 ml/1 level tbsp ghee
2.5 ml/½ level tsp cumin seeds
4 green cardamoms or 1 black cardamom
4 cloves

2.5 cm/1 inch stick cinnamon
1 bay leaf
6 whole black peppercorns
2.5 ml/½ level tsp salt
water

Put the rice in a sieve and wash it thoroughly under a running cold tap until the water runs clear. Soak in plenty of cold water for about 30 minutes. Drain the rice in a sieve and let it stand for a minute or two.

Heat the ghee in a large heavy-based saucepan. Add all the spices, fry for 1 minute, then add the rice and salt and level with a spatula.

Add enough water to cover the rice by about 2.5 cm (1 inch). Cover with a tight fitting lid, lower the heat and allow to cook for about 20 minutes until all the moisture has been absorbed and the rice is tender.

Gently fork the rice, working right down to the bottom. Transfer to a heated serving dish and serve immediately.

GUCHCHI KA PULLAO

Pullao with wild Kashmiri mushrooms

Guchchi are dried wild morels, fungi which grow in the mountains of Kashmir. As in Europe, morels are very expensive but they do have a distinctive flavour and are worth using for special occasions.

PREPARATION TIME: 10 MINUTES PLUS 30 MINUTES' SOAKING
COOKING TIME: 25 MINUTES   SERVES: 4–6

275 g/10 oz basmati rice
25 g/1 oz guchchi or 100 g/4 oz fresh mushrooms, sliced
30 ml/2 level tbsp ghee
1 medium onion, skinned and finely sliced

2.5 ml/½ level tsp black cumin seeds
2.5 ml/½ level tsp salt
1.25 ml/¼ level tsp chilli powder
water

Put the rice in a sieve and wash it thoroughly under a cold running tap until the water runs clear. Soak in plenty of cold water for about 30 minutes. Drain the rice in a sieve and let it stand for a minute or two. If using dried mushrooms, soak them in warm water for about 20 minutes. Drain and cut into 1.5 cm (½ inch) pieces.

Heat the ghee, add the onion and black cumin seeds. Stir-fry for 3–5 minutes until golden brown and crisp. Add the sliced mushrooms and stir-fry for a few seconds. Reduce the heat and stew for a

minute or two.

Add the rice to the stewed guchchi. Add the salt and chilli powder. Stir once to blend in all the ingredients. Level rice with a spatula and pour in enough water to cover it by about 2.5 cm (1 inch). Reduce the heat, cover and cook for about 20 minutes or until tender and all the moisture has been absorbed. Turn off the heat and let rice stand for a few minutes before lifting the lid. Gently fork the rice, working your way to the bottom. Tip rice into a heated serving dish and serve at once.

Palak poori and Chappati

HYDERABADI PUCKI BIRYANI

Hyderabadi cooked biryani

This unique 'cooked' biryani from Hyderabad is so called because both the meat and the rice are parcooked and then mixed together. To get the true flavour, the lid is sealed on with a dough paste to prevent any of the aromas from escaping. A distinctive feature of this biryani is its use of fresh or dried mint.

The meat is also first marinated in yogurt and spices, then cooked to almost tender, before being added to the parboiled rice. Instead of the two just being mixed together, they are placed in the saucepan in layers and left to finish cooking very gently: a rich dish.

PREPARATION TIME: 7¼ HOURS (INCLUDING MARINATING AND SOAKING TIMES)
COOKING TIME: 1–1¼ HOURS   SERVES: 6–8

1 kg/2 lb tender lamb (on the bone), cut into 5 cm/2
  inch pieces
2.5 cm/1 inch piece fresh ginger, peeled and finely
  chopped
2 garlic cloves, skinned and finely chopped
3 green chillies
175 g/6 oz ghee
225 g/8 oz onions, skinned and finely chopped
225 g/8 oz natural yogurt (dahi)
6 green cardamoms

6 cloves
5 cm/2 inch stick cinnamon
5 ml/1 level tsp black cumin seeds
small bunch each of fresh mint and coriander leaves,
  finely chopped
100 ml/4 fl oz fresh lemon juice
7.5 ml/1½ level tsp salt
450 g/1 lb basmati rice
1.4 litres/2½ pints water

Soak the meat in plenty of cold water for about 1 hour (this makes it a whiter colour when cooked). Meanwhile put the ginger, garlic and green chillies in a blender or food processor and grind to a fine paste. Drain meat, squeeze out any excess water and prick all over with a fork. Smear the ginger paste on to the meat and once again prick all over to ensure that it penetrates the meat. Cover and leave to marinate for half an hour.

Meanwhile, heat the ghee in a heavy-based saucepan and fry the onions for 5–10 minutes to a deep golden brown. Remove the onions from the ghee and stir in to the yogurt. Leave to marinate for about half an hour. Add the marinated meat to the yogurt along with the whole spices, the chopped mint and coriander leaves, lemon juice and the salt. Mix thoroughly, cover and leave to marinate for another 4–5 hours.

Reheat the ghee, add the meat and all the marinade, and, stirring frequently, fry the meat for 20–30 minutes until the meat is almost tender. Cover and allow to cook over low heat while the rice is being prepared.

Put the rice in a sieve and wash thoroughly under a running cold tap. In another pan, bring the water to the boil. Add the washed rice, bring it back to the boil and then let it cook for about 12 minutes so that it is parboiled. Drain and keep to one side.

If the biryani is to be cooked on the top of the stove, then remove the meat from the large pan but do not rinse it out. Place a 5 cm/2 inch layer of rice at the bottom, then a layer of meat on top, repeating this until the meat and rice has been used up. Pour in enough water to cover. *Do not stir.* Cover with a tight-fitting lid and allow to cook for another 20 minutes until the meat and rice are tender.

The same method applies to biryani cooked in an oven except that you add a little less water. Cook in the oven at 190°C (375°F) mark 5 for 35–40 minutes.

Once the dish is cooked, leave it covered for a few minutes. Then remove the lid, fluff up the rice with a fork and serve hot.

Nariyal ki chutney, Sonth, Dahi aur poodine ki chutney and Tamater ki chutney

JHINGE WALE CHAVAL

Prawn rice

The Arabian Sea yields king-sized prawns that are ideal for this kind of rice. However one may reconcile oneself to using smaller varieties of either fresh or frozen prawns. In this recipe I have used ordinary prawns which are added to the rice and cooked in the usual way.

PREPARATION TIME: 15–20 MINUTES PLUS 30 MINUTES' SOAKING
COOKING TIME: 25–30 MINUTES   SERVES: 4–6

275 g/10 oz basmati rice
15 ml/1 tbsp vegetable oil
1 medium onion, skinned and thinly sliced
2.5 ml/½ level tsp cumin seeds

100 g/4 oz fresh or frozen prawns, thawed
2.5 ml/½ level tsp salt
1.25 ml/¼ level tsp chilli powder
lemon wedge and coriander to garnish, optional water

Put the rice in a sieve and wash it thoroughly under a running cold tap until the water runs clear. Soak in plenty of cold water for about 30 minutes. Drain the rice in a sieve and let it stand for a minute or two.

Heat the oil in a large heavy-based saucepan. Add the cumin seeds. Stir-fry for 3–5 minutes until they turn a rich golden colour. Add the prawns and stir-fry for 2 minutes, then add the drained rice, salt and chilli powder.

Mix thoroughly and level rice with a spatula. Pour in enough water to cover the rice by about 2.5 cm (1 inch). Lower the heat, cover and cook for about 20 minutes until the rice is tender and all the moisture has been absorbed.

Fork the rice gently right to the bottom and transfer to a prawn or fish mould. Pat the rice into shape and carefully transfer to a heated serving dish. Garnish with lemon wedges and sprig coriander, if you wish.

GOSHT PULLAO

Meat pullao

Although at first glance the recipes for pullaos and biryanis may seem alike, they have very distinct flavours and personalities. Pullaos are the lighter and quicker versions of the biryanis, which are richer (in their fat content) and have more spices.

PREPARATION TIME: 20–25 MINUTES PLUS 30 MINUTES' SOAKING
COOKING TIME: 1½–2 HOURS   SERVES: 4–6

450 g/1 lb meat, such as lamb, on the bone, cut in
    4 cm/1½ pieces
4 cloves
5 ml/1 level tsp cumin seeds
2 green cardamoms
6 whole black peppercorns   } Tied in a
2.5 cm/1 inch stick cinnamon   piece of muslin
15 ml/1 level tbsp coriander seeds
3 small whole dried red chillies
7.5 ml/1½ level tsp salt
900 ml/1½ pints water
450 g/1 lb basmati rice

Masala
30 ml/2 level tbsp ghee
1 large onion, skinned and finely chopped
2.5 cm/1 inch piece fresh ginger, peeled and finely
    chopped
1 garlic clove, skinned and finely chopped
2.5 ml/½ level tsp chilli powder

rim most of the fat from the meat, wash thoroughly under a cold tap. Place the meat, spice bag, salt and water in a large, heavy-based saucepan. Bring to the boil and skim off any scum that rises to the top. Reduce the heat, cover and allow to boil gently for 1–1½ hours until the meat is really tender. Meanwhile, put the rice in a sieve and wash t thoroughly under a running cold tap until the water runs clear. Soak in plenty of cold water for 30 minutes. Drain in a sieve and let it stand for a minute or two. Strain the meat and reserve the stock. Discard the spice bag.

Prepare the masala. Heat the ghee in the heavy-based pan and add the onion, ginger and garlic and, stirring frequently, fry to a pale golden colour. Add the drained meat and chilli powder. Stirring frequently, fry this over medium heat for 5–10 minutes until the meat turns a rich golden colour.

While the meat is cooking, place the drained rice in a saucepan and add just enough of the reserved stock to barely cover the rice. Parboil for 10 minutes. Carefully add the rice to the browned meat and stir gently to mix all the ingredients. Add another 300 ml (½ pint) of remaining stock or water. Cover with a tight fitting lid, reduce the heat and allow to cook for another 7–10 minutes, until rice is tender. Fluff up the rice with a fork, then transfer it to a heated serving dish.

NAURATAN PULLAO

Mixed vegetable pullao

The Mogul emperor Akbar was renowned for his generosity and wisdom and for his able ministers. They were in fact known as the nine jewels – nauratan – that adorned his court and administration, and the grand chef at the court created many dishes in their honour. This term has lent itself to many kinds of art, one of them being the making of jewellery in which a piece with nine different jewels is said to be of a nauratan design. This pullao should traditionally be made with nine vegetables, apart from the rice, but you can choose as few or as many as you wish.

PREPARATION TIME: 15–20 MINUTES PLUS 30 MINUTES' SOAKING
COOKING TIME: 30–35 MINUTES   SERVES: 4–6

75 g/10 oz basmati rice
0 ml/2 level tbsp ghee
 medium onion, skinned and finely sliced
.5 ml/½ level tsp black cumin seeds
, green cardamoms
, cloves
.5 cm/1 inch stick cinnamon
 bay leaves

8 whole black peppercorns
225 g/8 oz mixed fresh vegetables (eg cauliflower, carrots, peas, mushrooms, French beans, turnips, peppers, tomatoes, okra) cut into small, equal-sized pieces
2.5 ml/½ level tsp salt
2.5 ml/½ level tsp chilli powder
water

Put the rice in a sieve and wash it thoroughly under a running cold tap until the water runs clear. Soak for 30 minutes in plenty of cold water. Drain the rice in a sieve and let it stand for a minute or two. Heat the ghee in a large heavy-based saucepan. Add the black cumin seeds, fry for a few seconds, then add the sliced onion and stir-fry for 3–5 minutes to a rich golden colour. Add all the whole spices and continue frying for another few seconds. Add the fresh or frozen prepared vegetables, the salt and chilli powder. Stir-fry for a further 1–2 minutes then reduce the heat, cover and allow to stew for 5 minutes.

Add the rice to the pan, stir gently to mix all the ingredients (do not stir too hard or the rice will break up). Level the rice with a spatula, add enough water to cover the rice by about 2.5 cm (1 inch). Reduce the heat to low, cover and cook undisturbed for about 20 minutes or until the water has been absorbed completely and the grains are separate.

Gently fork the rice, gradually working down to the bottom. Tip it into a heated dish and serve.

Bread

The origins of roti, unleavened wholemeal bread, can be traced back thousands of years and excavations have shown that many of the cooking implements used then were the same as those still being used today.

Unlike the western, commercial, mass-produced loaf, Pakistani bread is prepared fresh at each meal. All that is needed to make chappatis or parathas is an open fire and a tava, a cast-iron griddle. Nan is made in a tandoor. Most breads are made from wholemeal flour (atta). Exceptions include nan, bhatura and luchchi, which are based on plain flour. Special preparations such as cornmeal or millet bread are eaten on special occasions in certain parts of Pakistan, but the wholemeal roti or chappati remains a firm favourite.

The breads are flat – the nearest western equivalents are pitta bread or tortillas. With the exception of nan, they can be made in four different ways.

Chappatis

This type of bread is also known as roti or phulka in different parts of the country. A wholemeal flour and water dough is rolled into a thin, 10-cm (4-inch) round and then dry-roasted on a tava or in a cast-iron frying pan or griddle. These are the least fattening of Pakistani breads.

Plain parathas

The dough is exactly the same as for chappatis but is rolled out differently. Having rolled out the dough as for a chappati, a little ghee is smeared on the surface. The dough is then folded up in a similar way to puff pastry. It is divided into thirds. The first third is folded into the centre, then the other third is folded over, covering the first section. This way you are left with a rectangle of dough. A little more ghee is smeared over and the process repeated. The resulting small 'parcel' of dough is then rolled out to the required size and shallow-fried or dry cooked on the tava.

Stuffed parathas

The rolled out chappati is stuffed with a spicy mixture of meat or vegetables, then rolled out as for plain parathas, above, and shallow-fried.

Stuffed or plain pooris

This is plain or stuffed deep-fried bread. Proceed as for chappatis and then deep-fry them. For stuffed pooris, proceed as for the stuffed parathas, but instead of shallow frying, deep-fry them.

Bread-making equipment and techniques

Although no special implements are needed for making breads it is important to remember that the surface of the cooking vessel should be smooth. In Pakistan, a tava is used for making chappatis and parathas. Made of cast-iron, it is fairly heavy slightly concave in shape and has a smooth surface. A flat, heavy frying pan is a good substitute. Bread to be deep-fried can be cooked in any heavy, stable container that can hold oil, such as a deep-fat fryer or deep frying pan. In Pakistan, a karhai, which is shaped like a Chinese wok, is used. This is ideal for deep-frying because it uses less oil than a conventional deep fryer.

Nan is traditionally baked in a tandoor, a large unglazed, dome-shaped clay oven insulated with brick and mud to retain its heat. Live charcoal is placed at the bottom, where there is also an air vent. Once the walls of the oven are hot, the bread dough is slapped to stick on to the sides. It cooks within minutes and is removed with long metal tongs. Usually a little melted ghee and a few nigella seeds are sprinkled on top before the nan is served. Although nan can be baked in a conventional oven its taste and texture is not the same.

Most supermarkets or health food stores now sell wholemeal flour (atta), but it is also available in grocery stores, where it is even cheaper. Atta stores well in a cool, dry place and has all the high fibre content that is so essential for health. Stone-ground wheat, of course, has a better taste altogether than the milled variety. In Pakistan, village women often grind the daily requirement themselves on a stone mill called chakki, and even in urban households, people buy their wheat, clean it at home and take it to the local flour mill in the market to have the required amount of wheat milled especially for them.

It is very important to knead the dough really well to get it into a smooth, pliable consistency. Modern electric dough mixers or food processors do the job really well. If kneading by hand, then once the flour and water have been bound together, place the rough dough on a clean surface, shape your hand into a fist and knead it with that. Keep adding a few drops of water to moisten the surface of the dough. Then cover with a damp cloth or lid and leave to rest for 10–15 minutes, before beginning to roll out the dough and make the bread.

Doughs for breads such as nan are made of plain flour and are usually leavened with yeast, sour yogurt or a lump of fermented dough. This is then left to prove like dough for western bread before being baked in the tandoor.

CHAPPATI (ROTI OR PHULKA)

Wholewheat bread

Chappatis are the most common accompaniment to a Pakistani meal. They are healthy to eat, being made of wholewheat flour (atta) and dry roasted on a heavy griddle or tava. Many a newly married wife has suffered anguish while trying to make chappatis as they do need a bit of practice. Don't be disheartened if your initial attempts appear to be failures. Practice certainly makes perfect in the delicate art of chappati-making.

PREPARATION TIME: 5–7 MINUTES PLUS 15 MINUTES' RESTING
COOKING TIME: 15–20 MINUTES   MAKES: 8–10 CHAPPATIS

225 g/8 oz wholewheat flour
150–200 ml/5–7 fl oz tepid water

30 ml/2 level tbsp ghee

Place the flour in a bowl and mix in a little water at a time in order to bind the flour. Once all the water has been absorbed, place the dough on a clean, lightly-floured surface and knead it thoroughly with floured hands as you would for making ordinary bread dough. Once the dough feels fairly soft and pliable – the consistency should be like that of shortcrust pastry dough – replace it in the bowl. Cover with cling film or a piece of damp cloth and leave to rest for at least 15 minutes.

Heat a heavy frying pan, griddle or tava. Break off a small piece of dough and shape it in your palms into a smooth ball the size of a table tennis ball. Dip this into some dry flour in order to coat it. Place it on a clean, floured surface and roll it out into a round no more than 0.25 cm (⅛ inch) thick and about 12.5 cm (5 inches) in diameter. If the chappati tends to stick to the work surface, lift it carefully and dip into the flour once more.

Carefully place the rolled-out chappati onto the hot pan. As soon as small bubbles start to appear on the surface, turn it over, and repeat the process. Take a clean tea towel and carefully press down the edges of the chappati. This will not only make sure that the edges are cooked but also make the chappati puff up, making it light and fluffy. The chappati is cooked as soon as both sides have the brown spots on the surface.

Remove from the hot griddle or frying pan and smear with a little ghee or butter. Serve at once or keep warm in a clean tea towel or foil. Repeat with remaining dough.

Chappatis (both cooked and uncooked) freeze very successfully. If they are uncooked layer them between sheets of freezer paper, thaw them out slightly and cook in the normal way. If cooked chappatis have been frozen, there is no need to thaw them, simply put them straight under a hot grill and heat them through for a few minutes.

SADA PARATHA

Plain paratha

Basic paratha dough is similar to chappati dough and it is the addition of ghee or butter and the different ways of folding that give parathas their distinct character. Parathas come in three basic shapes: square, round and triangular. They are shallow-fried and crisp on the outside and soft inside. Cholesterol-conscious people can avoid shallow frying and simply dry-fry the parathas in a frying pan or on a griddle. Both methods are described below.

PREPARATION TIME: 10 MINUTES PLUS 15 MINUTES' RESTING
COOKING TIME: 20 MINUTES   MAKES: 8 PARATHAS

225 g/8 oz wholewheat flour
150 ml/5 fl oz water

45 ml/3 tbsp ghee

Square paratha

Put the flour in a bowl and add a little water at a time to bind it into a soft, pliable dough. Knead for a few minutes until the dough leaves the sides of the bowl absolutely clean. Cover with a cloth and leave to rest for 15 minutes.

Divide the dough into 8 equal parts. Place one portion in the palm of your hand and roll it into a smooth ball. Lightly coat it with a little dry flour and flatten it slightly on a floured surface. Roll out into a round of 10 cm (4 inches). Smear a little melted ghee on top. Fold ⅓ of the round into the centre and then the other ⅓ over the first fold so that you have a long rectangle measuring 2.5 cm (1 inch) × 10 cm (4 inches). Smear a little more ghee on this rectangle and repeat the folding, ⅓ up and ⅓ down, so that you now have a neat little square. Dip this square into dry flour to prevent it from sticking to the rolling surface. Roll out the paratha into a square no thicker than 5 mm (⅛ inch) and no larger than 12.5 cm (5 inches).

Heat a shallow, heavy frying pan or a griddle or tava. Test the heat by sprinkling a little dry flour on the hot surface: it should burn at once. Wipe the surface clean.

To dry-fry, lift the paratha and place it in the hot pan. Within a few seconds, small bubbles will start appearing on the surface and the paratha will become slightly opaque. Turn it over with a spatula and cook the other side. As soon as small bubbles appear on the surface the underside is cooked. Turn the paratha again and let the other side cook

again. Press down the edges with a clean cloth to ensure even cooking. Let the paratha cook for another few seconds then carefully remove it. Smear with ghee if you wish, or serve plain. Keep hot while you cook the remaining parathas.

If a crisp, shallow-fried paratha is preferred, then after the first turn, smear the top with a little ghee. Repeat the process each time you turn the bread to achieve a uniform crispness. Press down the edges using a spatula.

Round paratha

Roll out the dough into a large 15 cm (6 inch) round. Smear it with a thin layer of ghee. Then starting at the end nearest you, roll up the dough with your fingers into a long sausage shape. Carefully lift up the roll and place one end of it in the centre of your palm. Then carefully wind the rest of the roll around the centre point into a circle. Flatten the circle, coat with dry flour and carefully roll it out into a round no larger than 12.5 cm (5 inches). Proceed as for the square parathas (above).

Triangular paratha

Roll out the dough into a round no larger than 10 cm (4 inches). Smear a little ghee on the surface. Fold it in half. Smear a little more ghee on the top and once again, fold the dough in half, making a triangle. Roll out carefully to keep the shape. Proceed as for plain parathas.

AALOO KE PARATHE

Paratha stuffed with potatoes

Stuffed parathas are everyone's favourites. Often eaten for breakfast or brunch, they make a substantial meal in themselves. Various stuffings can be used but the most popular ones are either boiled mashed potatoes, finely shredded cauliflower or mooli or highly spiced minced meat. The basic method of making parathas is the same but the fillings have to be prepared in different ways, using different spices.

PREPARATION TIME: 15 MINUTES PLUS 15 MINUTES' RESTING
COOKING TIME: 45 MINUTES PLUS 20 MINUTES TO BOIL POTATOES
MAKES: 10–12 STUFFED PARATHAS

450 g/1 lb wholewheat flour
about 350 ml/12 fl oz water

Potato stuffing
30 ml/2 tbsp vegetable oil
5 ml/1 tsp ajowan seeds
1 medium onion, skinned and finely chopped
2.5 cm/1 inch piece fresh ginger, peeled and finely chopped

1 green chilli, finely chopped
450 g/1 lb potatoes, boiled in their skins, peeled and quartered
5 ml/1 level tsp ground coriander
2.5 ml/½ level tsp garam masala
2.5 ml/½ level tsp chilli powder
2.5 ml/½ level tsp dried mint leaves
7.5 ml/1½ level tsp salt

Prepare the dough. Put the flour in a bowl. Gradually add the water and bind the mixture into a soft, pliable dough. Knead well for a few minutes until the sides of the bowl are clean. Cover with a damp cloth or polythene bag and leave to rest for 15 minutes.

Meanwhile prepare the stuffing. Slice the potatoes very finely; set aside. In a shallow frying pan or karhai heat the oil, add the ajowan seeds. As soon as they pop, add the chopped onion, ginger and green chilli. Stirring frequently, fry them for about 10 minutes to a pale golden colour, then add the potatoes and the remaining spices, mint and salt. Increase the heat and, stirring and tossing continuously, fry the mixture until all the ingredients are well mixed. Remove from the heat and allow to cool completely.

Divide the dough into 10–12 equal parts. Shape each portion into a smooth ball. On a floured surface, roll out the ball to about 7.5 cm (3 inches) in diameter and place it in the palm of your hand. Place about 15 ml (1 tbsp) of the potato mixture in the centre of the dough and carefully fold up the edges to completely cover up the filling. Press the edges together to seal. Dip the stuffed ball into some dry flour to prevent it from sticking to the rolling surface and roll out into a round of no more than 15 cm (6 inches) in diameter.

Heat a heavy frying pan or a griddle or tava. Test the heat by sprinkling a little dry flour on the surface. The temperature is correct when the flour burns immediately. Wipe clean ready for use.

Carefully place the round of dough on the hot pan. Allow to cook for a minute then turn it over. Smear a little oil on the top and after a minute, turn it over again. The top side will now be covered with small brown spots. Spread some more oil on the surface and along the edges of the paratha. Turn it over again and repeat the oiling process. Press down the edges to ensure even cooking. Both sides of the paratha should be crisp. Remove from the pan and serve at once. (Parathas tend to become limp if they are kept standing around.) Repeat with remaining dough.

NOTE
If using mince then cook it to an absolutely dry consistency along with all the ingredients mentioned above, then proceed as in the above recipe.

MUTABAKH

Roti stuffed with mince

Various stuffings can be used for this recipe, vegetarian or non-vegetarian. Friends from Lahore often cook the vegetarian variety but the classic mince filling is equally delicious, although one paratha per person is more than enough.

PREPARATION TIME: 25 MINUTES   COOKING TIME: 1 HOUR   SERVES: 4

450 g/1 lb plain flour (maida)
5 ml/1 level tsp salt
100 g/4 oz melted ghee
a little tepid water
450 g/1 lb lean mince, with very little fat
8 black peppercorns, freshly milled

5 ml/1 level tsp cumin seed
2.5 cm/1 inch piece fresh ginger, peeled and finely
   chopped
1 green chilli, finely chopped
6 ml/1¼ level tsp salt
450 ml/¾ pint water

Sift the plain flour and salt into a bowl. Make a slight well in the centre and add 15 ml (1 tbsp) of the melted ghee. Using your fingers, mix it into the flour until it resembles dry bread crumbs. Add tepid water a little at a time and knead the flour into a soft pliable dough. Knead it thoroughly for a few minutes, then cover with a damp cloth and leave to rest for at least 30 minutes in a cool place.

Meanwhile place the mince along with the next five ingredients in a saucepan. Add the water and cook over low heat until the mince is tender and all the moisture has completely dried up. (This is extremely important as any trace of water will make it difficult to fry the paratha to the required crispness.) With a fork break up any lumps of mince. It should be really flaky. Leave to cool completely.

Break the dough into 12–14 portions. Roll each into a smooth ball, then roll each ball out into a round of about 20 cm (8 inches). Place the mince on top and spread it right to the edges. Cover the mince with another round of chappati and dampen the edges with a little water. Then press down the edges of the two chappatis firmly so that they do not open up during cooking.

Heat a tava or a large shallow frying pan. Carefully lift the mutabakh off the rolling surface and place it on the hot tava. Cook as for parathas (pages 54–55). Spread enough ghee on both sides to crisp up the paratha. Serve hot.

NAN

Leavened white bread

Anyone who has eaten in Pakistani restaurants is familiar with nan – the soft, flat pear-shaped bread. Nan is baked in a tandoor, a round, unglazed clay oven which is fired by live charcoal. It is the unique aroma of the clay and the coals that give nan its delicious taste. There are no racks in a tandoor, so the dough is slapped straight onto the inner walls of the hot tandoor. It sticks to the sides and bakes within minutes and is removed with long metal tongs. A conventional oven is not a bad alternative but the surface of the nan becomes more crusty than the soft supple ones baked in a tandoor, and the flavour is not the same.

PREPARATION TIME: 20 MINUTES PLUS 3 HOURS' PROVING
COOKING TIME: 10–15 MINUTES   MAKES: 8 NAN

325 g/12 oz strong plain flour
5 ml/1 level tsp baking powder
small pinch of bicarbonate of soda
5 ml/1 tsp salt
1 egg, lightly beaten

150 ml/¼ pint natural yogurt (dahi)
15 ml/1 tbsp vegetable oil
10 ml/2 level tsp sesame seeds (til)
10 ml/2 level tsp nigella seeds (kalonji)

Sift the flour into a bowl with the baking powder, bicarbonate of soda and the salt. Add the beaten egg and work it in with your fingers. Add the yogurt and oil and mix them into a fairly firm dough. (Add a little water if necessary as some yogurt is very thick.)

Knead well until the dough leaves the sides of the bowl clean. Continue kneading for another 5 minutes, then shape into a smooth ball. Put the dough back in the bowl, cover with a clean, damp cloth or polythene bag and leave in a warm place to rise (the airing cupboard is ideal) for about 3 hours or until the dough has doubled in size. Knead again for another minute or two then divide the dough into 8 equal portions.

Lightly grease several baking sheets. On a floured surface, lightly roll each portion out into an oblong about 15 cm (6 inches) long and about 7.5 cm (3 inches) wide, with tapering ends.

Brush the nans with a little cold water, sprinkle a few sesame seeds and nigella seeds on top and place in the oven at 200°C (400°F) mark 6 for 10–15 minutes until the top is pale golden in colour and crisp. To check that the nan is cooked, tap the underneath side as you would to check ordinary bread – it should sound hollow. Remove the nan from the baking sheets and serve at once.

POORI

Deep-fried wholemeal bread

Pooris are deep-fried chappatis. They absorb a fair amount of oil during cooking and can be a bit difficult to digest and are therefore much heavier than chappatis. Often served for Sunday lunch so that one can have a long siesta in the afternoon or at large gatherings as they are that much faster to fry.

PREPARATION TIME: 10 MINUTES PLUS 15 MINUTES' RESTING
COOKING TIME: 15 MINUTES   MAKES: 12–14 POORIS

225 g/8 oz wholewheat flour
10 ml/2 tbsp oil

150 ml/¼ pint tepid water
oil for deep frying

In a bowl mix together the flour and the oil. Pour in a little water at a time and bind the flour and oil into a stiffish dough (you may not need all the water). Knead the dough for a few minutes, then cover with a damp cloth and leave to rest for at least 15 minutes.

Heat the oil in a deep fat fryer or karhai. To test the temperature of the oil, drop a small piece of dough into it. It should float to the top at once. Divide the dough into 12–14 equal parts. Smear some oil on the palm of your hand and shape the dough between them into a smooth ball. Place the dough on a floured surface and roll out into a thin round no more than 10 cm (4 inch) in diameter.

Carefully lift a dough round and put it in the hot oil. With the edge of a slotted spoon, gently press the centre of the poori down into the oil. This helps the air to distribute evenly and allows the poori to puff up. As soon as the poori rises to the surface, turn it over to cook the other side. Gently press down the edges to ensure thorough and even cooking. Cook for a few more seconds then re-move the poori with a slotted spoon. Place on absorbent kitchen paper to drain and keep hot. Repeat with remaining dough and serve as soon as possible.

Accompaniments

There is a huge choice of pickles and chutneys in Pakistani cooking. Pickles are, on the whole, far more difficult to prepare than chutneys. They very often have to be left for days, if not weeks, to mature before they are ready to be eaten. Some of the pickle recipes require the ingredients to be blanched and steamed before spices and oils are added. A few pickles are prepared with meat, poultry and, indeed, fish.

In this chapter, I have concentrated on dishes that are both quick and easy to prepare. All sorts of fresh and dried ingredients are used, but the more popular ones include mint, tamarind, coconut and mango. The idea of serving a chutney or salad with the meal is to really get the digestive juices working and to increase your appetite.

The chutneys are not meant for long-term keeping. They will keep well for 2–3 weeks if stored in screw-topped jars in the refrigerator.

PYAZ AUR TAMATAR KA RAITA

Yogurt with onion and tomatoes

Make sure that the tomatoes you use for this recipe are firm so that they don't turn pulpy when mixed with the yogurt: a delicious combination.

PREPARATION TIME: 10 MINUTES PLUS CHILLING TIME   SERVES: 4–6

600 ml/1 pint natural yogurt (dahi)
2 firm tomatoes
1 medium onion, skinned and finely chopped
5 ml/1 level tsp dried mint

2.5 ml/½ level tsp garam masala (page 70)
2.5 ml/½ level tsp chilli powder
5 ml/1 level tsp salt

Leave yogurt to chill until required. Cut the tomatoes into quarters, remove the pulp and chop into small pieces. Add all the ingredients to the yogurt, mix well and serve.

SERVING SUGGESTION
Serve with any meal.

CHAAT

Spicy fruit and vegetable salad

Root vegetables such as potatoes and, in particular, sweet potato and dasheen, are used here along with salad vegetables and fruits. A delicious, highly attractive combination.

PREPARATION TIME: 30 MINUTES   COOKING TIME: 20 MINUTES   SERVES: 8

2 medium potatoes
1 medium sweet potato
1 medium or 4 small dasheen (arbi)
3 tomatoes
½ cucumber
2 apples
2 pears

2 oranges
2 bananas
7.5 ml/1½ level tsp salt
3.75 ml/¾ level tsp chilli powder
15 ml/1 level tbsp chaat masala (page 70)
juice of 2 lemons

Boil the potatoes, sweet potatoes and the dasheen in their skins. Drain and immerse in cold water to cool down quickly. Then peel and cut into medium-sized chunks.

Meanwhile, cut the tomatoes, cucumber, apples and pears into medium-sized chunks. Peel the oranges and cut each segment into half. Peel the bananas and slice into 1.5 cm (½ inch) thick slices.

Place all the prepared vegetables and fruits into a large bowl. Sprinkle on the salt, chilli powder and the chaat masala. Pour the lemon juice over the ingredients and really mix it in well with a spoon. Cover and chill slightly before serving.

DAHI BADE

Spicy pulse dumplings in yogurt

These dumplings are made of urad dal and appear in different guises all over Pakistan. The secret of making these dumplings is to beat the dal paste to incorporate a fair amount of air so that on frying they remain light and fluffy and do not become heavy and soggy.

PREPARATION TIME: 25–30 MINUTES PLUS OVERNIGHT SOAKING
COOKING TIME: 30 MINUTES   MAKES ABOUT 16 DUMPLINGS

225 g/8 oz split urad dal (with skins), thoroughly
  washed and soaked overnight

Stuffing
25 g/1 oz green raisins, soaked in warm water for 10
  minutes (kishmish)
1 medium onion, skinned and finely chopped
2 green chillies, finely chopped

30 ml/2 tbsp finely chopped fresh coriander leaves
oil for deep frying
600 ml/1 pint natural yogurt (dahi)
2.5 ml/½ level tsp chilli powder
1.25 ml/¼ level tsp freshly milled black pepper
5 ml/1 level tsp ground roasted cumin
5 ml/1 level tsp salt

Remove any dal skins that are floating on the surface of the water, using a slotted spoon. Rinse the dal a few more times to remove any more loose skins. If a few remain don't worry too much.

Place the soaked dal in a blender or food processor and grind to a smooth, thick paste. Add a little water at a time to ease the grinding. Test the dal between finger and thumb to check whether the grains can be felt. Continue grinding until all traces of the grain disappear. This will incorporate a fair amount of air and make the paste lighter in texture. To test if the paste is of the right consistency drop 5 ml (1 tsp) of the paste into a bowl of cold water. It should rise to the surface. If it sinks and remains at the bottom then the paste needs more beating. When the paste is ready, leave it to rest for a few minutes.

Prepare the stuffing. Drain the soaked raisins and squeeze out any excess water. Mix together the raisins, onion, green chillies and coriander leaves and keep aside. Heat the oil in a deep fat fryer or karhai. Test the temperature by dropping a small piece of paste into the hot fat. It should rise to the top at once.

Wet a large square of muslin and tie it securely over the top of a small bowl. Place about 15 ml (1 tbsp) of the paste on the wet muslin, wet your fingers and pat it into a round shape. Place a little of the stuffing in the centre and fold the paste in half over it, covering the stuffing completely. Turn the bowl upside down and carefully prise away the stuffed dumpling. Repeat with the remaining paste. Carefully lower the dumplings, a few at a time, into the hot oil. Fry to a golden colour, turning once or twice. Remove from the oil with a slotted spoon and place on absorbent kitchen paper. Repeat with the remaining dumplings.

Ten minutes before serving soak the dumplings in warm water to remove any excess fat. Press the dumplings between your palms carefully to squeeze out the water. Dip them in the yogurt and arrange them round the edge of a serving dish. Spoon the yogurt into the middle of the bowl. The reason for pouring the yogurt into the centre is to prevent the dumplings from soaking it all up. Sprinkle with the spices and salt and serve.

DAHI AUR POODINE KI CHUTNEY

Yogurt and mint chutney

PREPARATION TIME: 2–3 MINUTES   SERVES: 4

60 ml/4 tbsp natural yogurt (dahi)
15 ml/1 tbsp chopped fresh or 5 ml/1 level tsp dried
  mint

2.5 ml/½ level tsp chilli powder
2.5 ml/½ level tsp sugar
2.5 ml/½ level tsp salt

Mix all the ingredients together and chill slightly before serving.

SERVING SUGGESTION
A cooling chutney, serve with any meal.

TAMATER KI CHUTNEY

Tomato chutney

Various types of tomato chutneys are prepared all over Pakistan. Some are made with raw tomatoes, others with cooked ones. A few strands of saffron give this cooked chutney a special flavour.

PREPARATION TIME: 20 MINUTES   COOKING TIME 45 MINUTES   MAKES ABOUT 450 g/1 lb

450 g/1 lb very ripe tomatoes
225 g/8 oz sugar
150 ml/¼ pint water
2 garlic cloves, skinned and crushed
2 bay leaves
150 ml/¼ pint malt vinegar

25 g/1 oz green raisins (kishmish)
15 ml/1 level tbsp blanched almonds, chopped
5 ml/1 level tsp nigella seeds (kalonji)
2.5 ml/½ level tsp chilli powder
5 ml/1 level tsp salt
a very small pinch of saffron

Skin, then roughly chop the tomatoes. Dissolve the sugar in the water over a low heat.

Add the tomatoes, garlic, bay leaves and the remaining ingredients, except the saffron, to the sugar syrup. Reduce the heat and boil, stirring occasionally, for about 45 minutes, uncovered, until the tomatoes are reduced to a pulp.

Dissolve the saffron in 15 ml (1 tbsp) of water. Add it to the tomato mixture 10 minutes before the end of cooking. Stir well, then allow it to cool completely before storing in clean glass jars in a cool dry place. Keeps well for 2–3 weeks.

IMLI AUR POODINE KI CHUTNEY

Tamarind and mint chutney

The combination of tamarind and mint is absolutely delicious. Use either fresh or dried mint leaves.

PREPARATION TIME: 10 MINUTES PLUS 20 MINUTES' SOAKING
MAKES ABOUT: 100 g/¼ lb

50 g/2 oz tamarind
150 ml/¼ pint warm water
1 small onion, skinned
small bunch fresh mint leaves, chopped or 30 ml/2 tbsp
    dried mint

1 green chilli
5 ml/1 level tsp salt
2.5 ml/½ level tsp sugar
2.5 ml/½ level tsp chilli powder

Soak the tamarind in the warm water for about 20 minutes. Work the pulp loose with your fingers, then strain the liquid through a sieve into a glass or plastic bowl. With the back of a spoon, press down the tamarind to extract any extra pulp. Discard the residue in the sieve.

In a blender or food processor, finely grind the onion, mint leaves and the green chilli.

Mix together the tamarind juice, the ground onion mixture, salt, sugar and chilli powder. Chill slightly before serving.

Keeps well for 2–3 weeks.

KAYLE KA RAITA

Yogurt with bananas

A sweet and sour raita, this is a cooling counterpart to any fiery dish. It is traditionally served with sonth, the sweet and sour chutney in which the tamarind is toned down by the sweetness of jaggery.

PREPARATION TIME: 10 MINUTES PLUS CHILLING TIME   SERVES: 4–6

600 ml/1 pint natural yogurt (dahi)
3 large ripe bananas

2.5 ml/½ level tsp chilli powder
2.5 ml/½ level tsp salt

Leave the yogurt to chill until required. Peel and slice bananas into approximately 1 cm (¼ inch) slices. Add the bananas, chilli powder and salt to the yogurt. Mix carefully and serve.

Drinks

Pakistan is an intensely hot country for most of the year and many types of cooling drinks have been developed over the years to combat the heat. Lassi, a drink made from natural yogurt, is not only refreshing and cooling during the hot summer months but is also full of nourishment. Some people like it sweet, others like it salty. The list of variations is endless. Another cooling and refreshing drink is based on fresh lime or lemon juice which is diluted with ice cold water and flavoured sweet or salty, according to individual taste. Salty drinks are of course very important in a hot climate and need to be drunk regularly to replace salt in the body which is lost through perspiration.

Tea, of course, is a favourite drink all over the country. Pakistanis believe in spicing it up with cardamoms, cloves or cinnamon according to individual taste. So unlike the simple British cup of tea with milk, there are a number of variations to be tried.

NIMBOO PANI

Fresh lime drink

The tropical yellow and green limes (nimboo) are sharper and stronger than those available in the West. This is a favourite refreshing drink all around the year, but more so during the hot summer months. It is also a valuable source of vitamin C. You can make it savoury or sweet, with still water or soda. Ideal for slimmers.

PREPARATION TIME: 5 MINUTES   SERVES: 2–3

600 ml/1 pint cold water or soda
juice of 2 limes
3.75 ml/¾ level tsp salt

freshly ground black pepper
crushed ice
slices of lime to decorate

Mix together the water or soda, lime juice, salt and black pepper. Stir well to dissolve the salt.
   Add some crushed ice to the individual glasses, pour in the prepared drink, decorate with slices of lime and serve.

VARIATION

MEETHA NIMBOO PANI

Sweet fresh lime drink

Prepare as above, but omit salt and freshly ground black pepper and add 30–45 ml (2–3 tbsp) caster sugar.

PANNA

Saffron-flavoured mango juice

An absolutely delicious drink that is made from semi-ripe green mangoes. Choose large fruits as they are easier to handle. Prepare the concentrate first then dilute it when required.

PREPARATION TIME: 20 MINUTES   COOKING TIME: 20 MINUTES
MAKES ENOUGH FOR 20 DRINKS

4 large semi-ripe mangoes
60 ml/4 tbsp sugar

pinch of salt
a few strands of saffron

Press the mangoes all over to soften them, then spear with a fork and hold over a naked flame and, turning them over frequently, completely scorch the skins. Allow them to cool slightly for ease of handling, then peel off all the skin.
   Scrape the cooked pulp sticking to the large stone. Place in a blender or food processor. Add the sugar, salt and the saffron. Blend well. Store in clean glass jars in the refrigerator for up to 1 week.
   To serve, dilute to taste with chilled water (just as you would with orange squash).

LASSI

Yogurt drink

Lassi is quick and easy to make. It is also highly nourishing, refreshing and cooling and is a favourite all over Pakistan during the hot summer months. Lassi consists of diluted natural yogurt and can be flavoured with all sorts of whole or ground and roasted spices. It can be sweet or savoury and flavoured according to taste. I have given a few variations as a guideline after which you are free to experiment.

PREPARATION TIME: 5 MINUTES   SERVES: 4–6

Basic recipe
300 ml/½ pint natural yogurt (dahi)
900 ml/1½ pints cold water
3.75 ml/¾ level tsp salt
a little freshly ground black pepper
3.75 ml/¾ level tsp roasted ground cumin seeds
finely chopped fresh or dried mint, optional
crushed ice

Place all the ingredients except the crushed ice in a blender or food processor and mix together at high speed for 2–3 minutes.

Add some crushed ice to individual glasses, pour the prepared lassi on top and serve immediately.

VARIATIONS

Curry leaf and mustard seed garnish

5 ml/1 tsp vegetable oil
5 ml/1 level tsp mustard seeds
3–4 curry leaves

Prepare the lassi as above, omitting the cumin.

Heat the oil in a small pan, add the mustard seeds and the curry leaves. As soon as the seeds pop and splutter, pour this garnish over the lassi. Mix it in well and serve.

MEETHI LASSI

Sweet lassi

Prepare the Basic recipe, but omit the salt, pepper and the ground cumin seeds, and add 10–30 ml (2–3 tsp) sugar.

ALTERNATIVE FLAVOURINGS:
Flavour the sweet lassi with clear pale or dark coloured honey.

Spice the sweet lassi with a few finely ground green cardamom seeds or cinnamon powder.
Crunch the sweet lassi up slightly with finely chopped almonds and pistachio nuts.
Sharpen the sweet lassi by adding finely chopped fruit of your choice.

ILLAICHI WALI CHAI

Cardamom tea

A nice refreshing taste in your mouth is created by adding 2–3 green cardamoms to the teapot or 2.5 ml (½ tsp) ground cardamom seeds. Let it brew for 3–4 minutes then pour.

Desserts and Sweetmeats

Most Pakistani meals end with fresh fruit – mangoes, melons, watermelons, and so on. Desserts are usually kept for special occasions, such as weddings or religious festivals. Sweets play a very important part in the lives of all Pakistani people, and any excuse is found to eat these delicious concoctions. All good news is heralded with sweetmeats, so, for example to announce the birth of a son or an engagement, laddoos (small gram-flour droplets that are deep-fried and then steeped in syrup and shaped into balls) are distributed to relatives and friends. When a daughter is born burfi, a fudge made from thickened milk, is distributed, and so on. Sweets are mostly eaten at tea time, though in fact they are conjured up at almost any other time during the day as well. No matter if someone drops in at 11 o'clock in the morning, or 7 o'clock in the evening, a selection of sweets is always served with a steaming cup of tea.

Most Pakistani sweetmeats are fairly complicated and time consuming to make and, in fact, work out far more expensive when made at home than if bought from the sweet shops – methai wallahs. Some of the simpler sweets and puddings which will delight any palate are described in this chapter.

Pakistani sweets are generally milk-based and tend to be *very* sweet. In some recipes, the milk is first turned into paneer (soft cheese) and then deep-fried in ghee before being steeped or boiled in syrup, as with gulab jamun. In others, it is boiled down for hours until semi-solid or until it has been reduced by a half or more.

Almonds and pistachio nuts are important ingredients in Pakistani sweets, and are especially useful for decorating them. Rose water, cardamom seeds and saffron are often used to perfume the mixtures. One ingredient that is unique to Pakisanti cookery and which is not used anywhere else in the world (except in India) is varak, paper-thin sheets of beaten edible silver and gold. The sheets are spread on the finished sweets (and on festive meat or rice dishes). Varak is not only used as a decoration but also provides some of the essential minerals that the body needs.

PHIRINI

Cold rice flour milk pudding

This traditional Muslim dish is served on most festive occasions. Phirini is always served in little unglazed clay pots or deep saucers which are thrown away after use.

PREPARATION TIME: 5–10 MINUTES   COOKING TIME: 1–1¼ HOURS
COOLING TIME: 2½–3 HOURS   SERVES: 4

1.4 litres/2½ pints milk
75 g/3 oz coarse rice flour
100 g/4 oz sugar

25 g/1 oz blanched almonds, cut into slivers
5 ml/1 level tsp rose water
10 unsalted pistachio nuts, cut into slivers

Bring ¾ of the milk to the boil, then reduce the heat and let it simmer gently, uncovered. Dissolve the rice flour in the rest of the cold milk, then pour this mixture into the simmering milk. Stirring continuously, bring the milk to the boil then reduce the heat and simmer for about 1 hour, stirring frequently, until the rice flour is thoroughly cooked and the mixture has thickened to a thick pouring batter consistency, free from lumps. Add the sugar, slivered almonds and the rose water. Stir well to mix in the nuts and the flavour. Cook for a few more minutes until all excess moisture has evaporated and the sugar has completely dissolved. Pour the phirini into small individual serving dishes and decorate with the slivered pistachio nuts. Chill thoroughly for 2½ to 3 hours.

KHURMANI KA MEETHA

Apricot dessert

Use fresh apricots or dried ones if they are not available. I find that canned apricots do not give the same results.

PREPARATION TIME: 15 MINUTES   COOKING TIME: 40 MINUTES   SERVES: 4–6

450 g/1 lb fresh or dried apricots
900 ml/1½ pints water
225 g/8 oz sugar

50 g/2 oz blanched almonds, chopped
150 ml/¼ pint double cream, optional

If using fresh apricots stone them and cut into quarters. Place the fresh or dried apricots in a saucepan. Add 300 ml (½ pint) water, just enough to cover the apricots. Place the pan over low heat and allow the apricots to stew until they become pulpy. Meanwhile, dissolve the sugar in the remaining water and boil it down to two thirds of the original quantity.

Purée the apricots in a blender or food processor or rub through a sieve. Mix the apricot purée and syrup together and pour the mixture into a serving dish. Decorate with chopped almonds and chill thoroughly before serving. Serve with whipped cream.

GULAB JAMUN

Milk balls in syrup

Gulab jamun is one of the most popular sweets. Small balls made of milk powder are fried in ghee or clarified butter to a golden brown and then steeped in warm syrup perfumed with cardamoms and rose water to give a most delicious taste.

PREPARATION TIME: 15 MINUTES   COOKING TIME: 35–40 MINUTES   MAKES: 16–20

Syrup
450 g/1 lb granulated sugar
900 ml/1½ pints water
8–10 green cardamoms
10–15 ml/2–3 tsp of rose water
100 g/4 oz milk powder

40 g/1½ oz self-raising flour
10 ml/2 tsp semolina
10 ml/2 tsp ghee
about 60 ml/4 tbsp cold milk
ghee for deep frying

Make the syrup. Place the sugar, water, green cardamoms and rose water in a large saucepan. For this quantity a 3.4–4.5 litre (6–8 pint) pan would be ideal. Place the pan over gentle heat and let the sugar dissolve slowly. Increase the heat and boil for 5–8 minutes to make a syrup.

Mix together the milk powder, self-raising flour and the semolina. Melt the ghee and add it to the powder mixture. Work the ghee into the mixture with your finger tips so that it is well blended. Add a little milk at a time and bind the mixture into a smooth dough; the texture should be that of shortcrust pastry. Knead the pastry to eliminate any surface cracks. Break off small pieces of the dough and roll them into smooth balls. It is very important to make sure that no cracks are visible on the surface as these cracks may split open while frying; keep covered with kitchen paper to prevent drying during preparation.

Heat the oil or melt the ghee in a deep fat fryer. The temperature of the oil or ghee must not be very high as this will ruin the gulab jamuns. Carefully immerse milk balls into the warm fat. Keep moving them about with the perforated spoon or slice so that they fry evenly on all sides. The reason for frying them slowly is that they cook right through to the centre. If the ghee is too hot then the outside will brown too quickly and the centre will remain uncooked. Carefully strain the gulab jamuns with the slotted spoon or slice and at once immerse them in the warm syrup. Serve hot or cold.

SERVING SUGGESTION
Eat warm or leave for 3–4 hours and serve cold.

Lassi, Kayle ke chips, Panna, Samosas and Namkeen dal

KHEER

Rice pudding

Although Kheer is, in concept, similar to the English rice pudding, the method of cooking and the flavourings added to it are very different. The rice is simmered gently in plenty of milk until it becomes really soft and mushy and the milk has thickened to a creamy consistency. Nuts and dried fruits such as almonds, pistachio nuts, green raisins, spices such as green cardamoms and essences like rose water are then added to transform the humble rice pudding into something special.

PREPARATION TIME: 10–15 MINUTES   COOKING TIME: 1½–2 HOURS   SERVES: 4–6

0 g/2 oz rice, long grain or basmati
.4 litres/2½ pints milk
5 g/3 oz sugar
5 g/1 oz blanched almonds, cut into slivers

25 g/1 oz green raisins
25 g/1 oz unsalted pistachio nuts, cut into slivers
seeds of 3 green cardamoms, lightly crushed

Put the rice in a sieve and wash it thoroughly under running cold tap until the water runs clear. Drain and place in a heavy-based saucepan. Add the milk and bring to the boil over medium heat. Reduce the heat and, stirring frequently to prevent the rice from sticking to the bottom, simmer the pudding, uncovered, for 1½–2 hours until the rice turns soft and mushy and the milk has thickened (the consistency should be that of thick porridge). Add the sugar and, stirring continuously, dissolve it. This will also thicken the pudding slightly. Add the rest of the ingredients. Stir well and serve hot or cold.

KULFI

Ice cream

Kulfi is said to have been made in the Punjab long before ice cream ever became popular in the West. Nowadays it can be frozen in the freezer or ice cream maker though the shops specialising in kulfi still make it in the traditional way. The mixture is first poured into cone-shaped aluminium cases with a screw-on lid. These are then placed in a large round earthenware pot called a matka, which is full of ice and salt. The pot is then slowly rotated to help set the kulfi so that it does not get a chance to crystallize and the consistency is absolutely smooth and creamy.

COOKING TIME: ABOUT 1 HOUR
FREEZING TIME: SEVERAL HOURS OR OVERNIGHT   SERVES: 6

1.4 litres/2½ pints milk
15 ml/1 tbsp rice flour
175 g/6 oz sugar
50 g/2 oz ground almonds

150 ml/¼ pint double cream, lightly whipped
a few drops of rose water
25 g/1 oz unsalted pistachio nuts, cut into slivers

Pour the milk into a heavy-based saucepan and bring it to the boil, then reduce the heat and simmer briskly, uncovered, for about 45 minutes until it thickens and reduces to half its quantity. Remove from heat and allow to cool slightly. Dissolve the rice flour in a little of the thickened milk and pour it back into the pan. Over a low flame, stirring continuously, cook a further 15 minutes until the mixture thickens to a pouring batter consistency. Add the sugar and once again, stirring frequently, completely dissolve the sugar. Remove from heat, cover and leave it to cool down completely.

Add the almonds and mix into the mixture. Finally add the whipped cream, rose water and the slivered pistachio nuts.

Pour the mixture into a suitable container and place in the freezer. The important point to remember with kulfi is that you must take it out every hour and whisk thoroughly for the first 3 hours, then leave to set for several hours more or overnight. Allow Kulfi to soften for about 15 minutes before serving.

Kulfi and Aam wali ice cream

AAM WALI ICE CREAM

Mango ice cream

Mango, the king of fruit, unfortunately has a very short season during the hot summer months, though nowadays mangoes are imported from a number of countries ensuring a year-round supply. Canned mango slices or canned mango purée are now widely available.

PREPARATION TIME: 10 MINUTES   COOKING AND CHILLING TIME: 10 MINUTES   SERVES: 4–6

15 ml/1 level tbsp custard powder
45 ml/3 level tbsp caster sugar
450 ml/¾ pint milk
425 g/2 medium fresh mangoes, peeled and puréed or

15 oz can mango purée
100 g/¼ pint double cream, lightly whipped
sliced mango to decorate, optional

Mix together the custard powder and sugar in a saucepan. Pour in a little of the milk and dissolve the custard powder and sugar completely, then add remaining milk, stirring to make sure that no lumps remain. Place the saucepan over medium heat, and stirring continuously, bring the custard to the boil and thicken. Take care that it does not go lumpy. Remove from heat and immediately place the saucepan in a bowl of cold water and, stirring continuously, cool it down completely. Don't allow any skin to form on the surface of the custard.

When cold, fold the mango purée and the double cream into the custard. Pour the mixture into an ice cream maker and place the machine in the freezer and switch it on. (Then follow the manufacturers' instructions on how to get best results.) If there is no ice cream machine available, then pour the mixture into a suitable container, cover it and place it in the freezer. After every 20 minutes or so take the bowl out and give the mixture a good whisk with a rotary or balloon whisk. Repeat this at least 3–4 times. This will prevent any crystals from forming in the mixture. Take the ice cream out at least 10–15 minutes before serving to soften it slightly. Decorate with sliced mango, if you wish.

KASHMIRI ZARDA

Sweet saffron rice from Kashmir

Some of the world's best saffron comes from Kashmir and the delicate colour and aroma are essential to this dish.

PREPARATION TIME: 20 MINUTES PLUS OVERNIGHT SOAKING
COOKING TIME: 25–30 MINUTES   SERVES: 4–6

10–12 large strands of saffron soaked in 30 ml/2 tbsp
*   warm water*
225 g/8 oz basmati rice
1.25 ml/¼ level tsp salt
600 ml/1 pint water
75 g/3 oz granulated sugar
pinch freshly grated nutmeg (jaiphal)
seeds from 6 green cardamoms, crushed

30 ml/2 level tbsp ghee
4 cloves
2.5 cm/1 inch stick cinnamon
100 g/4 oz blanched almonds, cut into slivers
50 g/2 oz unsalted pistachio nuts, cut into slivers
25 g/1 oz green raisins, soaked and drained
15 ml/1 tbsp lemon juice

Infuse the saffron in the warm water. Rinse the rice in a sieve under the running water then soak it in cold water for 15 minutes. Drain and place in a large heavy-based saucepan. Add the saffron water and the salt. Then add 300 ml (½ pint) water. Bring to the boil, stir once, then cover with a tight fitting lid. Reduce the heat and cook for about 12–15 minutes until all the water has been absorbed. In a separate pan dissolve the sugar in the remaining water. Add the nutmeg and bring to the boil. Boil for two minutes, then remove from the heat.

Lightly crush the cardamom seeds. Heat the ghee and add the cardamom seeds, cloves, and the cinnamon. Stirring all the time, fry these for a couple of minutes. Stand well back, in case of spluttering, and add the syrup. Bring to the boil, then reduce the heat to low. Add the parboiled rice, cloves, cinnamon sticks, almonds, pistachio nuts, green raisins and the lemon juice. Stir just once, cover with a tight fitting lid and cook for another 10 minutes until the syrup is completely absorbed.

BADAM KI BURFI

Almond sweetmeat

This is a delicious sweet but it does take a lot of time to prepare. The almonds have first to be soaked overnight, then skinned and ground to a smooth paste with cold milk. This mixture is then slowly sautéed in ghee to arrive at the final result.

PREPARATION TIME: 45 MINUTES PLUS OVERNIGHT SOAKING   COOKING TIME: 1¼–1¾ HOURS
CHILLING TIME: SEVERAL HOURS OR OVERNIGHT   MAKES ABOUT 30

225 g/8 oz almonds
1.4 litres/2½ pints water (for soaking)
568 ml/1 pint cold milk
225 g/8 oz sugar

150 ml/¼ pint wate.
225 g/8 oz ghee
silver leaf (varak) or halved almonds for decoration,
  optional

Soak the almonds in the water overnight. They should be puffed up and double in size the next day. Skin the almonds and place them in a blender or food processor. Grind them to a smooth paste on a low speed, adding the milk gradually. Do not grind the almonds first on their own and then add the milk as too much of the almond oil will get lost.

In a heavy-based pan dissolve the sugar in the water, boil it rapidly for about 10 minutes to half its quantity. Add the ground almond paste and, stirring very frequently, simmer the mixture for 1¼ hours until it thickens. At no stage should it be allowed to stick to the bottom and scorch, as that will ruin the taste of the fudge.

In another pan, melt the ghee. Slowly pour a little ghee into the almond paste and, stirring continuously, see that it is absorbed completely into the paste. Within a few minutes the paste will start releasing the ghee. As soon as that happens, pour in a little more ghee and, once again stirring continuously, see that the ghee has been absorbed. Repeat this process until all the ghee has been used up and the rich almond paste is glossy.

Transfer the paste to a thali or a shallow 28 × 18 × 3 cm (11 × 7 × ¼ inch) cake tin and spread it out into a thickness of no more than 1.5 cm (½ inch). Leave it to cool down. As soon as it begins to set, cut it into squares or diamonds and leave it to cool completely for several hours or overnight. Decorate with silver leaf or halved almonds if wished. Lift off the fudge with a spatula and arrange on a serving dish.

GAJJAR KA HALVA

Sweet carrot halva

One of the most popular puddings of Punjab, this is made in most households during the winter months when carrots are plentiful. The grated carrots are simmered for 2 hours in milk and then fried in a little ghee, then almonds, pistachios, green raisins and some crushed green cardamom seeds are added. Decorate the halva with silver leaf (varak) for a special occasion.

PREPARATION TIME: 25–30 MINUTES   COOKING TIME: 2½ HOURS   SERVES: 6–8

900 g/2 lb fresh carrots, peeled and coarsely grated
1.7 litres/3 pints milk
100 g/4 oz granulated sugar
50 g/2 oz ghee
50 g/2 oz blanched almonds, cut into slices

25 g/1 oz unsalted pistachio nuts, cut into slivers
25 g/1 oz green raisins
seeds of 6 green cardamoms, crushed
Silver leaf (varak) for decoration, optional

Put the grated carrots in a large heavy-based saucepan and add the milk. Simmer, uncovered, over low heat, for 2 hours. Keep scraping the sides of the pan to loosen any coagulated milk that may stick there and add this to the carrots to help to thicken the milk in the pan. Keep stirring and scraping the pan until nearly all the milk has evaporated.

Sprinkle in the sugar and mix it in really well. Stirring frequently, cook the carrots for 30 minutes, uncovered, until all the water from the sugar has evaporated and the carrots begin to stick to the bottom of the pan. Add the ghee, almonds, pistachios, raisins and the crushed cardamom seeds. Stirring continuously, fry the mixture until the ghee is first absorbed by the carrots and then released. The halva is ready when the ghee begins to separate and has a glossy shine. Transfer to a serving dish and decorate with silver leaf. Serve hot or cold.

Basic Recipes

GHEE

Clarified butter

Before the days of refrigeration, a traditional way of preserving milk was to churn it into butter and then clarify it into ghee. By clarifying the butter the chance of it quickly going rancid is eliminated. Although ready-made pure butter ghee is available in most oriental grocery stores, it is a very expensive commodity. Ghee can be easily made at home by buying the cheapest brand of slightly salted butter. It can be stored indefinitely in the refrigerator.

Ghee making reminds me of an incident while I was at college and I was showing my teacher and classmates how to make ghee. All went well until we strained it through a nylon sieve and into a plastic container. Imagine my horror and shock when the hot ghee poured all over the table as the nylon and plastic melted into great big holes and we all were left to mop up the mess. Make sure you use a metal sieve and a porcelain or pottery bowl when straining ghee.

PREPARATION TIME: 2 MINUTES   COOKING TIME: 15 MINUTES   MAKES ABOUT 175 g (6 oz)

225 g/8 oz slightly salted or unsalted butter

Place the butter in a heavy-based saucepan. Melt it over medium heat and simmer until a thick froth appears. Let the butter simmer gently until the froth starts to separate from the clear golden liquid and some of the sediment settles at the bottom. Simmer for another minute or two but keep watching the ghee carefully as you don't want it to overbrown.

Remove from the heat and leave it to cool down slightly. Put a piece of muslin or a double layer of absorbent kitchen paper inside a sieve and place the sieve over a glass storage jar or other non-plastic container and carefully pour in the ghee without disturbing any of the sediment at the bottom of the pan. Allow to cool and cover tightly with foil or cling film.

DAHI

Yogurt

Yogurt is one of the easiest things to make at home and does not, in fact, require any special gadgets or expensive investment. All you really need is a heat-proof bowl or a wide-necked vaccum flask and a whisk or spoon. The best place to set the yogurt is the airing cupboard, wrapped up well in old towels or a teacosy. It will take about 8 hours to set.

PREPARATION TIME: 10–15 MINUTES   SETTING TIME: OVERNIGHT OR 8–10 HOURS
MAKES: 600 ml/1 PINT YOGURT

568 ml/1 pint milk   *10 ml/2 tbsp natural yogurt (dahi)*

Pour the milk into a saucepan. Bring to the boil then leave to cool to blood temperature (to test the temperature, dip a clean finger into the milk. It should not feel too hot or too cold but just comfortable). Pour the milk into a warmed bowl or vacuum flask. Add the yogurt and whisk in well. If using a bowl, cover with cling film then wrap in a towel and place in a warm place. If using a flask, close securely. Leave the yogurt undisturbed overnight or for 8–10 hours until set. Do not move the container in the meantime or it won't set. As soon as the yogurt has set, refrigerate and use as required.

NARIYAL KA DOODH

Coconut milk

All sorts of delicious alcoholic and non-alcoholic cocktails can be made using coconut water.

Using a fresh coconut

PREPARATION TIME: 10–35 MINUTES

MAKES ABOUT 150 ml/¼ PINT COCONUT MILK

Flesh of one large coconut, grated

150 ml/¼ pint water

To *make thick coconut milk*, add 100 ml/4 fl oz water to the grated coconut and leave to soak for 15–20 minutes. To extract the milk, squeeze out the grated coconut into a bowl with clean hands. Squeeze again to extract more milk, which will be thinner than the first.

To *make thin coconut milk*, add 150 ml/¼ pint water to the squeezed grated coconut and leave to soak for 10–15 minutes. Squeeze again to extract more milk which will be thinner in consistency.

Using creamed coconut

Slabs of commercially produced solid creamed coconut can be brought in most ethnic stores and larger supermarkets. To make up thick coconut milk, just dissolve the creamed coconut in some warm water. For thin coconut milk, just increase the amount of water.

MAKES ABOUT 150 ml/¼ PINT THICK COCONUT MILK

150 ml/¼ pint warm water
50 g/2 oz creamed coconut

Pour the warm water over the coconut and stir continuously to dissolve. Use as required.

IMLI KA RUS

Tamarind juice

PREPARATION TIME: 20 MINUTES

MAKES ABOUT 175 ml/6 fl oz TAMARIND JUICE

50 g/2 oz tamarind pods

150 ml/¼ pint warm water

Soak the tamarind pods in the warm water for about 15 minutes to soften and loosen the pulp. Strain through a sieve and press down the tamarind with a spoon to extract as much of the pulp as possible. Discard the pulp and use the juice as required.

PANEER

Soft cheese

The homemade cheese called paneer is a way of preserving milk in a hot climate. It takes very little time to prepare and is immediately ready for use in savouries, snacks, sweets and puddings. Nowadays, you can buy ready made paneer in slabs, but I find it more convenient to make it at home.

PREPARATION TIME: 10 MINUTES

MAKES ABOUT 175 g/6 oz PANEER

1 litre/2¼ pints milk

about 20 ml/4 tbsp fresh lemon juice or 22.5 ml/4½ tsp vinegar or 2.5/½ tsp acetic acid

Bring the milk to the boil, then remove from the heat and add lemon juice, vinegar or acetic acid until the milk begins to separate. Give the milk a stir and it will separate into paneer (cheese) and whey. Let it stand for a few minutes to coagulate, then strain through a piece of muslin placed over a sieve. The whey can be used instead of water in sauces. Use the paneer as required.

PRESSED PANEER
Flatten the paneer on a plate until 2.5 cm (1 inch) thick, wrap it in a clean cloth or in muslin and weight it down for several hours or overnight. Cut into shapes and use as required.

Spice mixtures

Some of the following spice mixtures need to be ground up fine before being used in recipes. The easiest way to do this is in an electric food mill – a small coffee grinder is ideal, or a mortar and pestle can be used as an alternative. If using a coffee mill, make sure you wipe it thoroughly before and after use with a clean, dry cloth. Grinding up a few slices of bread helps get rid of any lingering aroma of coffee or spices as well.

Only make up small quantities of spice powder and aim for a fast turnover, for they soon lose their flavour and aroma if stored too long.

PANCH FORAN

Five spices

Just at the Chinese have a favourite five-spice mixture, similarly the Bengalis have their own five-spice blend. The spices can be mixed whole or ground into a fine powder. The best way is to keep a ready-mixed blend handy and grind small quantities to powder as and when required.

25 g/1 oz cumin seeds
25 g/1 oz nigella seeds (kalonji)
25 g/1 oz aniseed (sauf)

25 g/1 oz fenugreek seeds (methi seeds)
25 g/1 oz brown mustard seeds

CHAAT MASALA

A delicious mixture of lightly roasted spices that are ground together. Commercially produced chaat masala can also be bought from most stores.

15 ml/1 level tbsp cumin seeds
15 ml/1 level tbsp coriander seeds

4 whole dried red chillies
5 ml/1 level tsp whole black peppercorns

Lightly dry-roast all the spices in a small frying pan. As soon as the cumin and coriander seeds start to colour slightly and pop and splutter remove from heat and grind into a fine powder in a small electric mill. Store in an airtight container.

GARAM MASALA

The literal translation of garam masala is 'warm spices'. There are two types of hot spices, of course: those which cause a nice, warm feeling in the body and those which burn your tongue. It is the first category that we are concerned with here.

Various types of garam masala are produced all over the sub-continent. For example, the one produced in the north is a simple one using up to 7 spices, whereas one from Hyderabad in southern India uses as many as 10 or 15 spices. Which type you use also depends on whether the mixture is to be used for vegetarian or non-vegetarian food, and, of course, on individual taste. Ready ground garam masala is easily available in all sorts of shops, but because ground spices rapidly lose their essential oils and flavours it is advisable to buy in small quantities as a last resort, or better still, make your own at home. The recipe below is intended as a guide and the quantity of any spices can be decreased or increased, according to taste.

15 ml/1 level tbsp whole black pepper
10 ml/2 level tsp cumin seeds
2.5 cm/1 inch stick cinnamon

4 black cardamoms or 10 green cardamoms
5 ml/1 level tsp cloves
3 bay leaves

Crush the black cardamoms thoroughly before adding them to the other spices as they are very hard and may ruin the blades of your blender. In a small electric mill, grind all the spices to a fine powder. Store in an airtight container.

PAPAD

Poppadoms

These thin, round, crisp wafer-like discs are very difficult to make at home, so it is best to buy the dried ready made varieties from oriental stores and supermarkets and finish off the cooking at home.

There are several different types of poppadoms. Some are made from rice flour and come either plain or flavoured with red or green chillies. Others are made out of various dal flours and are usually flavoured with chillies and black peppercorns.

Poppadoms can be shallow-fried in oil or grilled. I think the fried ones have a slightly better flavour, but the grilled ones are better for the weight conscious.

Frying method
Heat 1.9 cm (¾ inch) vegetable oil in a large frying pan and cook each poppadom over medium heat until bubbles appear on the surface and they puff up and turn golden brown. (This takes seconds; do not allow to burn as this spoils the taste.) Remove with a draining spoon, then place on absorbent kitchen paper. Serve as soon as possible.

Grilling method
Place one poppadom at a time on grill rack about 5–7.5 cm (2–3 inch) under a medium flame. Grill until bubbles appear on the surface and the poppadom is evenly golden. (Watch carefully as it will expand in seconds.) Turn the poppadom over and cook for a further 5–10 seconds. Serve as soon as possible.

ATTE KI LAIP

Dough paste

Dough paste is often used in traditional Pakistani cookery to completely seal a pot and prevent any steam from escaping during cooking. This method of cooking is known as dum.

The paste is usually made of wholemeal flour and water mixed together to a sticky dough. These days, of course, it is easier for us to put a double layer of kitchen foil over the pan and top it with the lid for the same effect.

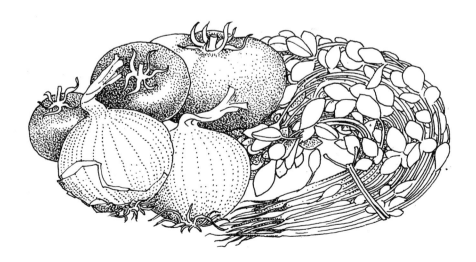

Glossary

This section is intended as an introduction to ingredients which are used in Pakistani cookery and which have been used in this book – everything from herbs and spices to fruits, vegetables, flours and oils.

Spices

For the purpose of this book, and with a few exceptions, I have classified spices as being the dried seeds or other parts of plants, and herbs as the fresh, leafy ones.

STORING SPICES
Spices are the dried seeds, leaves or bark of trees and plants and it is essential that they are allowed to breathe. Store whole or ground spices in glass jars in the dark or in opaque containers which are not absolutely airtight. Although spice racks with pretty bottles do look very attractive in a kitchen they do nothing for the spices, for strong light causes them to lose their colour and, in time, their essential oils as well. Ground spices tend to lose their flavour, aroma and colour much faster and should only be bought in small quantities.

To save time, or on occasions when green chillies, root ginger and garlic are plentiful and cheap, buy them in bulk and either grind them together or separately to a paste in a blender or food processor and freeze in ice-cube trays. Once frozen, they can be removed from the trays and stored in polythene bags and put back in the freezer. One large ice cube is equivalent to 15 ml (1 tbsp) of chopped raw ingredients, and an average recipe for 4 people will require 15 ml (1 tbsp) of the mixture.

Ajowan
Although ajowan does not have an equivalent name in English, it is often sold under its botanical name *carum*. It belongs to the caraway and cumin family and has small, distinctive light brown seeds. A spice with digestive properties, it is often used to alleviate minor stomach aches and with foods that cause flatulence.

Allspice (kebab cheeni)
A unique spice which tastes of cloves, cinnamon and nutmeg. Jamaica is the world's largest supplier of allspice. The medium-sized berries are picked while still green and then dried in the sun until they turn a dark brown.

Aniseed or fennel seeds (saunf)
An aromatic and digestive spice with distinct, elongated seeds that are a pale green or very light brown. Its taste and smell are very similar to liquorice. Aniseed is most commonly used in the Bengali and Kashmiri-style cooking, where it is either used whole or ground into a fine powder. Often chewed after a meal to aid digestion or brewed in tea to cure mild colds.

Asafoetida (hing)
Neither seed nor a true plant, this is derived from the resin of a plant grown mainly in Iran and Afghanistan. Asafoetida can be bought in solid form (but it is very hard and can damage the blades of your grinding machine) or as a powder in small tins, which is more convenient to use. It has an extremely interesting flavour and aroma when used in minute quantities in cooking, but produces a very pungent smell when the box is first opened (the smell is due to the presence of sulphur compounds). It counteracts flatulence and is always added to pulses, beans and green vegetables.

Black pepper (kali mirch)
Black pepper is a traditional ingredient in the preparation of medicines in the Indian Ayurvedic system. A digestive and stimulant, it also enhances the flavour of any dish to which it is added.

It is considered to be a 'warm' spice and as such is an essential ingredient of Garam masala (page 70). Good quality black pepper should be free of dust and stalks and you should not be able to crush it between the nails. Always use freshly ground black pepper.

Cardamoms (illaichi)
India is the home of cardamoms of both the small, green (chotee illaichi) and large, black (badi illaichi) cardamoms. (White cardamoms have less flavour as they have been bleached. I feel they are inferior to green cardamoms and do not recommend them.)

Cardamoms, green
Good-quality green cardamoms should be pale in colour and firm to the touch. The seeds inside should be black or dark brown and slightly sticky with a white membrane surrounding them. The husk as well as the seeds are used in cooking both sweet and savoury dishes; the flavour is pungent and highly aromatic. Cardamom is a digestive spice and is often chewed after a meal. It also has medicinal properties and helps to alleviate nausea and when brewed with tea and other spices helps to

clear sore throats and colds. Cardamom is one of the 5 'warm' spices and is an essential ingredient of Garam masala (page 70).

Cardamoms, black
Although these belong to the same family as green cardamoms, they are larger in size, coarser in texture and in taste. Often used in meat, poultry, and rice dishes and in the making of Garam masala (page 70) and Spiced Tea (page 62). Unlike green cardamoms, they are not suitable for eating raw as they have a slightly bitter taste and a very strong flavour.

Chillies
Chillies vary in colour and shape. They are generally sold either green (unripe) or red (dried), or in a powder form in tins.

Green chillies (hari mirch)
Fresh chillies should be firm and shiny. They come in all sorts of shapes and sizes and different shades of green. Often eaten raw as an accompaniment to the meal, they can be lethally sharp. It is the tiny seeds that cause the fiery sensation and not so much the skin, which, in fact, has a very pleasant flavour.

In most of the recipes in this book where whole chillies are called for, they are specified as, for example, '2 green chillies'. If it is flavour you are after rather than heat, then slit the chilli, *remove the seeds* and rub a little salt inside. Then wash thoroughly. Always wash your hands after handling chillies and keep them well away from your eyes.

Fresh green chillies can be stored, unwashed, in a plastic bag in the salad drawer of the refrigerator.

Red chillies (lal mirch)
Dried red chillies are sold whole or ground. The effect of chilli powder is that much more concentrated and so it is used in minute quantities.

Cinnamon (dalchini)
Cinnamon is the bark of a tree grown in the tropical forests of Sri Lanka, south India and other Asian countries. In fact, the bark of two different trees is often sold under the name of cinnamon.

True cinnamon is recognised by the beautiful quills sold in most supermarkets.

Coarse, dark bark from the cassia tree, which grows in India, is also sold as cinnamon. Although cassia bark is not as attractive in appearance as the cinnamon quills, I find that it has a much stronger flavour. Only a very small piece is needed to flavour a dish. Cinnamon is a 'warm' spice and is an essential ingredient in Garam masala (page 70).

Cloves (lavang)
Cloves are dried flower buds from evergreen trees which grow in profusion in the monsoon forests all along the southern coast of India. Good cloves should be well formed, plump and oily.

Cloves have analgesic qualities as anyone who has suffered from toothache will know. The essential oil extracted from cloves is a good remedy for toothaches, but if this is not available, then just chew one or two cloves. They are also used in pickles as a preservative and are an essential ingredient in Garam masala (page 70).

Coriander seeds (sookha dhania–kotmir)
The seeds are used as a spice and the fresh green leaves as a herb (page 74). The mature, round, light brown seeds are easy to split into two but quite difficult to grind into a fine powder unless you persevere with a mortar and pestle or a spice mill. The small seeds are more aromatic when lightly dry roasted and ground into a fine powder.

Cumin (jeera)
Cumin, must not be confused with caraway (which is never used in Pakistani cooking); it comes in two varieties:

White cumin (sufaid jeera)
The true flavour and aroma of this spice emerges after it is added to hot oil or after it has been dry roasted. Cumin fried in oil forms the basis of many dishes, whereas dry-roasted ground cumin (bhoona jeera) is used as a seasoning or garnish (especially for yogurt dishes) rather than in cooking. The temperature of the fat is crucial when cooking with cumin. If it is not hot enough the seeds will not splutter and pop and will not release all their flavour. Instead they will become hard and brittle without any flavour. An essential ingredient in making Garam masala (page 70).

Black cumin (kala jeera)
Black cumin is a highly aromatic spice and should be used in small quantities. It is most commonly used in rich meat and poultry dishes and is an essential ingredient for making the rich biryanis.

Fenugreek (methi dana or methre)
Another versatile plant in which the fresh leaves are used as a herb (page 74) and the dried seeds as a spice. Fenugreek seeds are small, rectangular light brown or mustard-coloured seeds. They are extremely hard and are mostly used whole as they are difficult to grind into a powder at home. Fenugreek seeds are an acquired taste as they are very bitter; fry them until they are dark brown in colour to help remove some of the bitterness. I find it is best to literally burn them, then cool and strain the oil, discard the bitter seeds and reuse the flavoured oil.

Ginger, dry (sonth)
Ginger is often referred to as both a herb and as a spice. I prefer to describe fresh root ginger as a herb (page 75) and the dried whole or powdered ginger, as a spice.

Mace (javetri)
Both mace and nutmeg are obtained from the same tree. The fruit of the tree is the colour and size of a small peach, whose kernel, nutmeg, is surrounded by a scarlet, open-weave case (the aril), which is known as mace. Small amounts of mace are used in both Hyderabadi and Kashmiri cooking, usually in non-vegetarian food.

Mango powder (aamchoor)
Segments of unripe mango are dried in the sun then either used whole or ground. Adds a piquant, slightly sour tang to savoury dishes.

Mustard seeds (rai or sarson)
Mustard belongs to the spinach family and is used as a green vegetable in Punjab. There are three varieties of mustard seeds, black, brown or Indian mustard, and white (alba) mustard. To obtain the full flavour of the seeds, they must be fried quickly in very hot oil.

Nigella seeds (kalonji)
Small, triangular shaped, hard black seeds that belong to the onion family. Very often confused with, and referred to, as black cumin. The two spices have nothing in common and must never be substituted for one another.

Poppy seeds (khus khus)
Tiny, cream-coloured, slightly nutty tasting seeds which have a cooling effect when ground and used. The Indian poppy plant is cultivated and the seeds are used in savoury dishes as well as sweet. Also acts as a thickener.

Saffron (zaffran or kesar)
Saffron is the dried stamens of a crocus. The most expensive spice in the world which, it is said, was worth its weight in gold: between 70–75,000 flowers are required to produce 450 g (1 pound) of saffron.

Saffron is a highly aromatic spice and gives a delicate yellow-orange colour to any dish. A pinch is often enough to colour a fair amount of food and too much saffron will very often ruin a dish. Turmeric must never be used in place of saffron.

Sesame seeds (gingelly or til)
Creamy white, small, almond-shaped seeds with a nutty flavour. Natives of India, sesame seeds are also grown in China and other sub-tropical countries.

Turmeric (haldi)
It is colourful and leaves its mark on whatever foodstuff it is added to. It has digestive, preservative and antiseptic properties.

A small amount of turmeric is enough to flavour and colour the dish; too much makes the food bitter. Never use turmeric if saffron is called for.

Herbs

Unlike in Western-style cooking in which a large variety of fresh and dried herbs are used, Pakistani cooking uses a very limited amount.

Basil (tulsi)
Although a widely used herb in continental cooking, basil is hardly ever used in Pakistani cooking. The only exception to the rule is when a few leaves are brewed with some spices in medicinal teas.

Bay leaf (tej patta)
Tej patta is the leaf of the cassia tree (whose corky bark is often sold as cinnamon) but bay leaves make a good substitute. Choose tender, young leaves as they are full of flavour. Usually used in meat, poultry, fish and rice preparations.

Coriander leaves (hara dhania or kotmir)
The fragrant, aromatic green leaves of the coriander plant are used as a garnish. It is one of the oldest herbs used for cooking. Coriander is an easy plant to grow and will flourish in almost any soil – it will even grow in a window box. It releases its flavour when the leaves are crushed or chopped.

STORING FRESH CORIANDER
Bunches of coriander leaves are usually sold with the roots intact. Cut off the roots and any tough stalks. Wash the remaining stalks and leaves thoroughly under a cold tap and carefully remove all traces of mud. Allow to dry thoroughly on absorbent kitchen paper, then loosely pack in a plastic bag and refrigerate until required. Fresh coriander can be frozen but tends to go black, so the leaves and stems are only suitable for cooking but not garnishing.

Curry leaves (curry patta, meetha neem)
Thin, shiny, dark green leaves with the distinct 'curry' flavour of the commercially produced 'curry powder'. Do not confuse curry leaves with bay leaves (above) as the two have nothing in common. The best aroma is released when they are lightly fried in hot oil for a few seconds.

Fenugreek leaves (hari methi)
Fenugreek leaves, which are sold fresh or dried, have a slightly bitter flavour. They are used as a herb and a vegetable and the dried seeds as a spice. Remove the tough stalks, chop the leaves and lightly sauté in oil with potatoes.

Garlic (lasun)
Some classify garlic as a spice, others as a herb. It has a pungent flavour and should be used in moderation as a flavouring agent. Garlic is considered to have medicinal properties and be good for the blood.

Never fry garlic in fat or oil which is too hot or it will burn and develop an unpleasant, acrid flavour.

Fresh ginger (adrak)
Ginger comes from the rootlike stems or rhizomes of a tropical plant. Root ginger consists of pale brown gnarled stems which slightly resemble Jerusalem artichokes in appearance. Buy only plump, firm ginger. Carefully scrape or peel off the skin and then cut as required.

Fruit and Vegetables

Aubergines (baingan)
Natives of India and now grown in various parts of the world, aubergines come in various shades of pink, purple, green and white and in varying sizes and shapes. The flesh inside is soft and white with tiny edible seeds. Has endless uses, as fritters, roasted, stuffed and lightly sautéed, to name a few. Small, young aubergines can be cut up and used straight away, while larger ones should be cut up, lightly salted and left in a colander or sieve for about 30 minutes to drain off bitter juices. The pieces are then rinsed and patted dry.

Bananas, green (kache kayle)
Unripe green bananas are used in a variety of delicious savoury and sweet dishes. Finely sliced deep fried banana chips are a favourite snack (page 8).

Bitter gourd (karele)
There are many different varieties, shapes and sizes of bitter gourd. Some of them look a bit like cucumbers with bright green, knobbly skins. The flesh inside is white with medium-sized edible seeds.

Chickpeas, green (cholia)
Fresh green chickpeas are usually sold as part of the plant on which they grow. Green chickpeas are harvested long before they reach maturity and are then allowed to become yellow and hard (channa).

Coconut (nariyal)
A hard, dark brown fruit with crisp, snow-white edible flesh. On the sub-continent there is a special device for grating fresh coconut but, as this implement is not always readily available, I find it easy to grate the coconut on a hand grater or electric food processor. For information about making coconut milk, see page 69.

Dasheen (arbi)
A dark brown, thin-skinned vegetable. Since it produces a sticky extract when cooked, it is best to boil dasheen in its skin first and then peel it before adding it to a dish.

Green raisins (kishmish)
Usually imported into Pakistan from Afghanistan, these delicately coloured, subtly perfumed fruits are dried, seedless, sweet green grapes. Don't use dark raisins instead, as the colour, texture and taste are totally different. They are used in both sweet and savoury dishes and are sold in good quality grocery stores.

Guava (amrood)
A delicious, delicately scented fruit, light creamy yellow on the outside with a thin, edible skin and creamy or delicate pink flesh with small, hard seeds.

Jackfruit (kathal)
A huge, green, prickly-skinned fruit that can weigh up to about 32 kg (about 70 lb). Eaten both as a vegetable and a fruit. The thick skin is inedible and is peeled to reveal creamy-white, segmented flesh with large, soft, edible seeds. The seeds of mature jackfruit harden and have to be discarded and the fruit itself becomes sweet and has a sickly sweet odour.

Okra (bhindi)
As its common name, 'ladies' fingers' suggests okra resemble the perfect, tapered fingers of a well-formed hand. The pods are green with white flesh and small, edible seeds. They release a sticky extract which disappears on cooking. Simply wipe clean with a damp cloth, cut off the stalk and use as indicated in recipes.

Lotus stems (bhain, nadroo)
Lotus is a sacred plant in India and China and grows wild in water throughout certain parts of Asia. A speciality of Kashmir, lotus stems can be bought here fresh or canned. This vegetable has an off-white, hard, fibrous stem and has five hollow chambers and looks beautiful when cut across. The stem is cut into the required lengths, quickly boiled in lightly salted water and then used as required.

Lychee
A delicately perfumed fruit that has a rosy pink, slightly knobbly, inedible skin and pulpy white flesh with one or two large inedible seeds.

Mango (aam)
The mango is grown in the tropical and sub-tropical regions of the world. It has anything from a green, yellow to pinkish red skin and the soft, orange-yellow flesh is very similar to a peach, both in colour and texture: the large kernel is discarded.

The taste of mangoes varies, according to variety, some can be very sweet and perfumed, others have a sharper tang. Unripe mangoes are used for chutneys and pickles. Mango slices and purée are available in cans; although they cannot be compared to the fresh mangoes they are a good substitute.

Marrow (ghia)
Many different types of marrow are available, and often one can be substituted for another. They range from fairly small, pale green-skinned vegetables to giants with dark green skins.

Mooli
A member of the radish family, this is a long, white, tube-shaped vegetable which can be grated and eaten raw, or made into a stuffing for parathas.

Mushrooms (khumba)
Cultivated white mushrooms are just becoming popular in Pakistan. Guchchi, popular but very expensive wild morels which are native to Kashmir are used in special rice dishes (page 48).

Mustard greens (Sarson ka saag)
A member of the spinach family; the leaves of the mustard plant are popular vegetables with the Punjabi community in Pakistan, where the plant is grown in abundance. Cook as spinach.

Papaya (papita)
A delicious, soft-fleshed fruit with a green or yellowy-orange skin when ripe and delicately perfumed soft, orange-pink flesh with a mass of tiny, black inedible seeds. Excellent for keeping the stomach in order. Widely eaten for breakfast with a squeeze of lemon juice. Unripe papaya is often used as a meat tenderiser.

Peas, green (mattar)
Pakistani peas are the same as those found in Europe but we also use the shells. They are snapped at one corner and pulled along the length to remove tough transparent layer (like stringing beans). The shells are then chopped into small pieces or kept whole. Use as for beans.

Pomegranate (anaar)
A beautiful pink-red, hard skinned fruit which, when cut open, reveals a pinkish red honeycomb structure inside. The delicious seeds fit into this honeycomb and are encased in a bitter white membrane. Prise seeds away and discard the rest. The seeds and pulp can be eaten raw.

Sweet potatoes (shakarkandi)
A member of the potato family, this dark, pink skinned vegetable is cooked like ordinary potatoes. Has a slightly musky or nutty flavour, ideal in salads.

Tinda
A member of the marrow family, resembling tiny round cucumbers with pale green skin and soft white flesh with edible seeds. Delicious stuffed.

Yam (jimikandh)
A large, tuberous root vegetable with dirty brown skin and off-white or pale pink, hard flesh. When cooked, it has a bland flavour and is best peeled and cooked in a spicy sauce.

Flavouring ingredients

Almonds (badam)
A native of the Mediterranean, small amounts of almonds are grown in Pakistan. These have a slightly bitter taste when compared to the western sweet almonds. Used in sweet and savoury dishes.

Betel nuts (areca, supari)
A hard nut that grows on trees resembling the coconut palm. The small nut in its untreated state is slightly poisonous. As the nut is a stimulant it is often added to betel leaf and chewed after a meal.

Chirongi nuts (cuddapah almonds)
Small rounded nuts that resemble large whole Egyptian lentils both in colour and size. A musky flavoured nut, it is used in Hyderabadi cooking.

Cocum
Even after having looked up countless books, I have not been able to find an English name for this ingredient. Cocum is a variety of plum which is pitted and then dried. They resemble prunes but have a more pronounced, sour flavour.

Jaggery (gurd)
Derived from cane, jaggery is a light brown lump of unrefined sugar and has a unique musky flavour. Refined sugar cannot really be used instead but use soft dark brown sugar as a substitute.

Melon seeds (char magaz)
Melon seeds are used as a flavouring in some Pakistani dishes and although they are available shelled and unshelled in some ethnic shops. Next time you buy some melons, keep the seeds, place them in a sieve and wash them under a running cold tap. Gently rub the seeds to remove any pulp still sticking to them, then spread them out on a piece of newspaper or absorbent kitchen paper to dry off completely. Once dry, shell them by pressing them open (using tweezers, if you like) at the tapering end of the seed; discard the shells and spread the kernels out to dry thoroughly. Store in a dry, screw-topped jar.

Pine nuts (Chilgoze or nioze)
Small, long, creamy-coloured nuts with a thin dark brown shell. Eaten raw and used in cooking.

Pistachio nuts (pista)
Natives of Afghanistan and Iran, pistachios have a hard, creamy white shell and pale green kernel. Can be eaten roasted and salted. The unroasted and unsalted variety is finely chopped and used in both savoury and sweet dishes.

Pounded rice (poha)
Pounded rice should not be confused with flaked rice, which is obtainable in most grocery stores. Pounded rice is husked and stewed, then flattened. It is excellent for making quick savoury snacks.

Tamarind (imli)
A large pod or bean that grows on enormous shady trees in India. Tamarind is seeded, peeled and pressed into a pulp which is used to add a sour flavouring in savoury dishes and for making chutney. For information on how to make tamarind juice, see page 69.

Yogurt (dahi)

Yogurt has long been acknowledged as an essential component of a well-balanced diet. It is a delicious, nutritious, easily digestible and an extremely versatile derivative of milk. No Pakistani meal is complete without a dish of yogurt, either plain or with another flavouring added to it.

Yogurt can be made from the milk of ewes, buffaloes, goats or cows. It is soured with lactic bacteria which coagulate the liquid, giving it a thick, pleasant texture and a milky, acidic taste.

No expensive gadgets or special equipment is needed to make homemade yogurt. A pottery bowl, or, in fact, a bowl with a lid, that will retain the heat is all that is necessary. See page 68 for how to make homemade yogurt.

Pulses (dals)

Although there are hundreds of different types of pulses, lentils and beans, I am going to give a brief description of the ones used in this book and as there are very few equivalent English names, I have used the Pakistani names first. Use of a pressure cooker cuts down overall cooking time of all these ingredients dramatically.

Channa dal
This dal is very often confused with split yellow peas. Although they belong to the same family that is where the similarity ends. Channa dal is the husked, split, black chickpea. It is deep yellow in colour and has an irregular surface. A high protein dal with a slightly nutty flavour.

Kabli channe (white chickpeas)
A hard, creamy white pea which, when soaked, doubles in size. Often used in Mediterranean cooking. Thoroughly boiled first and then used as required in salads, stews and in a spicy sauce.

Kale channe (black chickpeas)
Although of the same family as white chickpeas, these have a hard, dark brown skin and are smaller in size. They need thorough soaking before being boiled. Then used as required. The boiled liquid makes an excellent soup as black chickpeas have a high protein content.

Lobhia (black-eyed beans)
Creamy white, large oblong beans with literally a black 'eye' in the middle. Black-eyed beans need 4–5 hours soaking; they have a musky flavour.

Moong or mung dal
Each one tastes different and requires different lengths of time to cook. Three types of moong dal are available:

SABAAT MOONG (*whole moong beans*)
A tough little bean that is not normally soaked. It is boiled in plenty of lightly salted water until the skin splits and the bean is tender. Most people prefer these beans to be cooked until mushy, but that is individual taste.

MOONG DAL CHILKE WALI (*split moong beans with skins*)
These need to be soaked for about 1 hour, and then boiled in spiced water until tender. They take less time to cook than saabat moong (whole moong beans).

DHOOLI HUI MOONG DAL (*washed moong dal*)
Split moong beans with their skins removed. This pale yellow dal needs very little soaking and cooking time and is light and easy to digest. Highly recommended for children and old people.

Moong dal is often soaked and ground, then formed into small balls or dumplings and deep fried; these are then either steeped in natural yogurt or in a spicy sauce or they may be tossed in salt and spices and eaten as a snack.

Masoor (Egyptian lentils)
Like the Moong bean these lentils come in two varieties:

SAABAT MASOOR (*whole lentils*)
A dark brown or pale green skinned flat bean which takes a fair amount of time to cook (best done in a pressure cooker). A delicately flavoured lentil with a pale, pinky orange centre.

MASOOR DAL (*split Egyptian lentils*)
These pinkish lentils are quick to cook and require very little soaking. Often used in lentil soup.

Moath
Small, elongated brown beans with a strong, nutty

flavour. They do require prolonged cooking to become tender. Can be cooked to a dry consistency with spices or to a thick, soup-like consistency.

Rajma (red kidney beans)
These large, deep maroon beans have a slight nutty flavour.

Red kidney beans contain a poisonous resin that is not destroyed by light boiling. Therefore, to be on the safe side, they should be first soaked for a minimum of 8–10 hours until they have doubled in size. They must then be *boiled* for at least 10 minutes, before cooking as specified in recipes.

Toovar (arhar or toor) dal
A split mustard yellow bean that is commercially oiled. Easy to cook with a light, nutty taste.

Urad dal
These can be divided into three categories. Urad is a tough, shiny black bean the size of moong beans, with a musky flavour. It is heavy on the stomach and needs added spices to aid digestion.

SAABAT URAD (maa)
Whole urad, which require long cooking for the skin to split and the bean to tenderise.

URAD DAL CHILKE WALI (split urad dal, with skins)
These take less time to cook than the whole urad. Also releases a glutinous liquid which gives the cooked dal a creamy consistency.

DHULI HUI URAD DAL (washed split dal, without skins)
Requires even less cooking but needs to be soaked for about 1 hour prior to cooking. Often ground into a paste and fried into fritters or balls.

Flours

All sorts of ingredients are ground into flour in Pakistani cooking, such as channa dal, moong dal, urad dal, rice and corn.

Cornmeal (makki ka atta)
Used to make the traditional bread from Punjab in Northern Pakistan. Similar to tortillas of Mexico.

Gram flour (besan)
Widely used flour in a variety of dishes. It also acts as an emulsifier when added to yogurt and prevents it from curdling during cooking.

Moong and Urad dal flour (dal ka atta)
Both flours are used for savoury pancakes and for savoury snacks and dumplings.

Rice flour (chaval ka atta)
Fine-ground rice flour is used for savoury pancakes and for sweet milk puddings such as phirini.

Roasted chickpea flour
This must not be confused with gram flour (besan). Black chickpeas are first roasted then skinned and the pea ground into a fine powder. This flour has a musky taste which not only enhances the flavour of a dish but also acts as a thickening agent.

Oils and Essences

Pakistani cuisine varies from one region to another, and the cooking medium used differs as well.

Ghee (clarified butter)
One traditional method of preserving milk was to churn it into butter and then clarify it. Clarified butter is not only less likely to go rancid after a while but can also be heated to high temperature without risk of burning.

Ghee can be easily made at home (see page 68 for recipe). Vegetable ghee is also available in tins but is a much cheaper, inferior product to pure butter ghee.

Groundnut oil (moongphali ka tail)
Grounds (or peanuts or monkey nuts) are a rich source of protein and oil. They are highly valued for their virtually colourless and odourless oil.

Kewra (screwpine)
Kewra trees bear highly fragrant flowers similar to that of roses. It is used to flavour and perfume both sweet and savoury dishes.

Mustard oil (sarson ka tail)
The oil is pressed from the mustard seed and has a rich, pungent smell and taste and is deep gold in colour. To remove the odour and some of the pungency in cooking, mustard oil is always heated almost to smoking point, then cooled down to the right temperature for use.

Sesame oil (gingelly or til ka tail)
Sesame is a native of India but is now cultivated in other parts of the world. Indian sesame oil is a light colourless oil. It must not be confused with Chinese sesame oil, which is extracted from roasted sesame seeds and consequently darker in colour and heavier.

Rose water (gulab ka pani)
Rose water and artificially flavoured concentrates are used to flavour desserts and sweetmeats.

Varak (silver leaf)
To make varak, tiny pellets of silver or gold are placed between sheets of tissue paper, enclosed in a leather pouch and then beaten with a heavy, metal hammer. This effectively flattens the pellets into paper-thin sheets.

Index